EXTREME DISTANCE
Paper
Airplanes

New Designs for Ultra Long-Range Flights!

TAKUO TODA

TUTTLE Publishing

Tokyo | Rutland, Vermont | Singapore

DART SERIES

SPEAR PLANE 14

LANCER ZERO 16

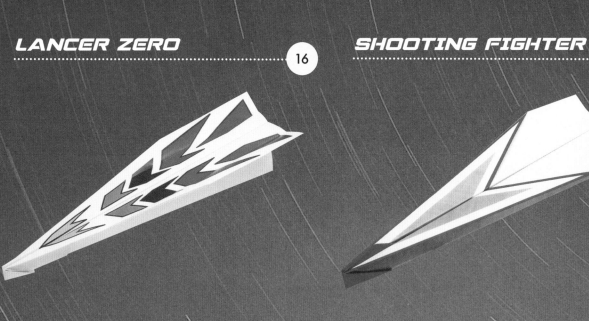

SHOOTING FIGHTER 18

ARROW FIGHTER 20

LANCER 23

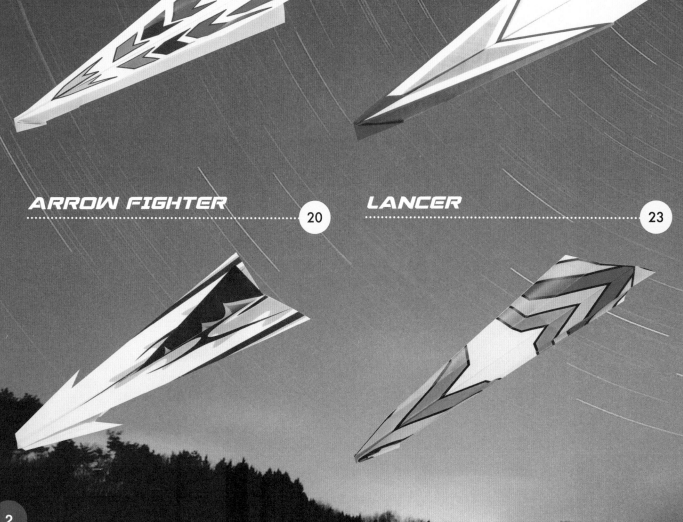

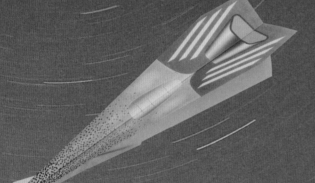

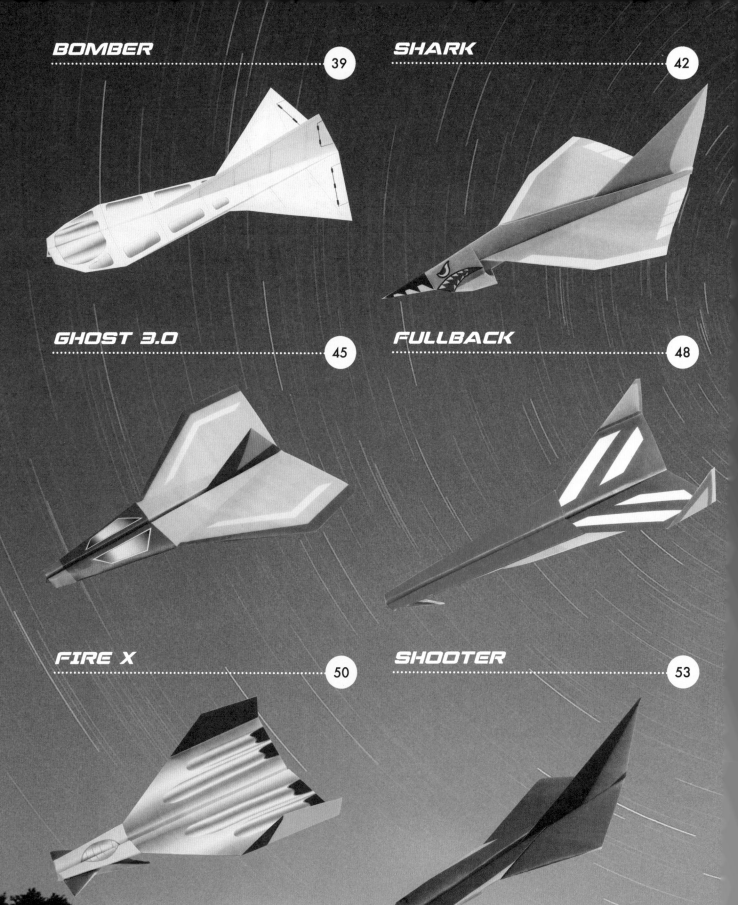

LONG PLANE
.... 56

SUPER PLANE
.... 58

AIR KING
.... 60

Longest flight distance in Japan!

Fly paper airplanes that are expertly tailored for long-distance flights! There's even one that holds the record for the longest-flight distance in Japan.

Why I Wrote This Book

It's so disappointing when the paper airplane you took the time to make just twirls around and quickly nosedives without flying a satisfying distance. How can you make it fly better and farther?

Paper airplanes—particularly the long-distance type—are less likely to veer off to the left or right and are easier to fly more or less horizontally if the overall length of the fuselage is longer than the width of the wings. However, if you make it too long and thin like a rocket, it will only fly with the momentum of the throw without much glide time, like a javelin's trajectory arc. By finding the optimal balance between the width of the wings, the length of the fuselage, and the center of gravity, you can create a paper airplane that flies straight and far.

A folded paper airplane, which lacks an engine or any power source, is more accurately described as a "glider" rather than an airplane. The flight length is dependent on how well the wings can catch the air and glide. To fold planes that yield longer flights, you first need to understand how to create a plane with a distortion-free, streamlined fuselage and finely adjusted wings. Also, throwing the paper airplane with just the right amount of acceleration, rather than relying on brute force, will make a significant difference in how far it flies. This book will show you how to select suitable paper for your paper airplanes, make fuselage adjustments, and throw the planes effectively.

This book showcases a varied collection of long-distance type airplanes that are relatively easy to fold. There are cool-looking airplanes, interesting configurations, and many new and advanced designs—including one special model that holds Japan's longest flight distance record!

By using the information in this book, your airplanes will catch the air and fly straight, level and far. I hope that you enjoy making these fun paper airplanes!

—Takuo Toda,
Chairman of the Japan Origami Airplane Association

—Nobuaki Fujiwara,
Director General of the Japan Origami Airplane Association and Holder of the Japanese Distance Record for Paper Airplanes

The Folding Symbols Used in This Book

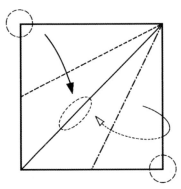 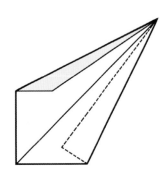 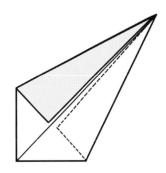

——————————— Paper edges

 Fold toward the front side

- - - - - - - - - - - Valley fold line (after folding, it's hidden inside)

 Fold toward the back side

— · — · — · — · — Mountain fold line (after folding, it remains outside)

 Flip the entire paper over

————————— Crease line (indicated only when necessary)

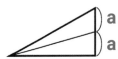 Indicates spans of equal length

 Reference point

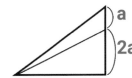 Indicates a span of twice the length

 Reference line

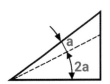 Indicates that the degrees of angle 2a are twice those of angle a

Fold Inside

① Fold in half.

② Fold only the top layer and return it.

③ Reverse the crease made in step 2 into a mountain fold.

④ Fold to the inside.

⑤ Complete.

 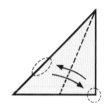 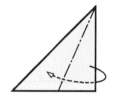 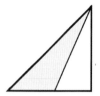

Inside-Reverse Fold

① Starting from the state of Fold Inside step 5 (above), make a crease and unfold.

② For segment AC (top layer), make a mountain fold, and for segment AD (bottom paper), make a valley fold.

③ Open the paper slightly and fold by pushing segment AB toward the inside.

④ Complete.

 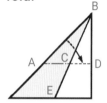 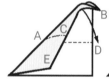 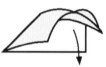 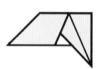

Double Inside-Reverse Fold

① Starting from the state of Fold Inside step 5 (top), make a crease, and then fold the top layer back at an angle.

② Return to the original state.

③ Perform an inside-reverse fold along the AB segment.

④ Perform another inside-reverse fold in the opposite direction along the AC segment.

⑤ Complete.

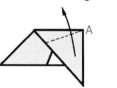 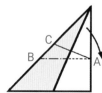 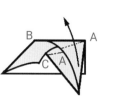 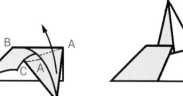

How to Make Firm, Accurate Creases

Your results will vary, depending on the size of the paper and the direction in which it's being folded.

1 ▶ Take hold of the bottom left corner and lift it, bringing it toward the top left corner.

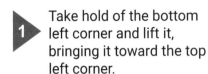

2 ▶ Once the top left corners are aligned, keep your right hand still and withdraw your left hand.

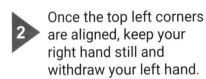

3 ▶ Gently flatten the bottom left corner of the paper with your left hand.

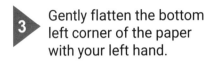

4 ▶ While pressing down firmly on the bottom left corner with the tips of your left-hand fingers, release your right hand.

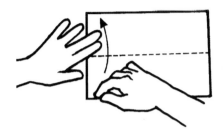

5 ▶ Take hold of the upper right corner and pull it toward the direction of the arrow, aligning the edges of the paper.

6 ▶ With your left pinky finger as the anchor, crease the bottom left half by spreading the other fingers.

7 ▶ Keep pressing down on the paper with the tips of your left-hand fingers while you release your right hand.

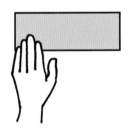

8 ▶ Gently hold down the bottom right portion with your right hand and lightly make a crease.

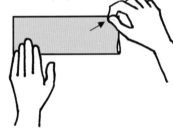

9 ▶ With the pad of your right thumb, make a strong crease on the bottom right half of the paper.

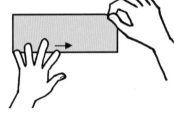

10 ▶ Do the same on the bottom left to complete the crease.

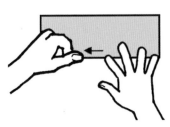

Folding with a Ruler

When folding along a line connecting two widely spaced points, it's convenient to use a ruler. Also, when the paper is thick and hard to fold because of multiple layers, applying a ruler can make it easier to fold.

① Identify the landmarks.

② Align the ruler with the two points.

③ Run your fingernail along the edge to make the crease.

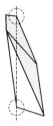

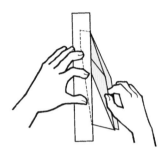

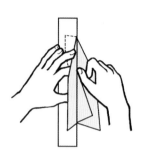

Selecting Paper Suitable for Paper Airplanes

• For *glider* types (planes that stay aloft for a long time) and paper airplanes with complex folds: use smooth, lightweight/thin A4 size (8.27 in × 11.69 in / 21 cm × 29.7 cm) copy paper.

Paper with a shiny surface is not suitable for paper airplanes because it is thin and heavy. Furthermore, for paper airplanes that require complex folds, thin and slightly stiff paper is preferable. Stiff paper doesn't bulge at the creases due to the paper's elasticity when folded, and it has the strength to withstand the stress of strong throws.

The stiffness of the paper can be determined by how it droops, as shown in Figure 1. The more you handle paper, the more it absorbs oils and moisture from your hands, making the paper lose its crispness. When folding paper airplanes, try to fold with your fingertips instead of pressing with the palm of your hand to reduce the transfer of moisture.

• For *distance* types (planes that fly far—the subject of this book): use slightly heavier-weight/thicker A4 size (8.27 in × 11.69 in / 21 cm × 29.7 cm) copy paper.

Figure 1

Fold with your fingertips instead of pressing with the palm of your hand to avoid the transfer of moisture.

How to Adjust Your Plane Before Flying It

Proper adjustment will make your airplane fly better. Remember the following adjustment techniques and the correct way to throw the airplane that suits its design.

1 ▶ Correcting Twists in the Airplane

First, look at the airplane from the front to check if the wings have any significant twists. If the wings are twisted or bulging, the airplane won't fly well. For wings with a lot of twist, place them on the edge of a desk and straighten them by "burnishing" from above with a ruler or similar object.

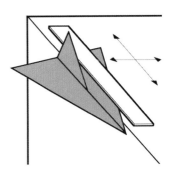

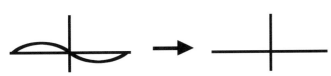

2 ▶ Adding Elevators

Elevators are the horizontal control surfaces at the back of the plane that affect lift. To emulate them on your paper airplane, twist the rear of the wings slightly upward by a little less than ¼ inch (6 mm), as if you're lifting them with your fingernails. Having elevators will significantly improve the airplane's performance, and the dimples tend to help the wing layers stay together.

Side view

It's best to hold the airplane at a point that's one-third of the distance from the nose of the plane.

3 ▶ Test the Effect of the Elevators

Gently throw the airplane with a motion that pushes it straight out away from you, aiming about 5 degrees downward. Don't snap your wrist, but throw it almost like you would throw a dart.

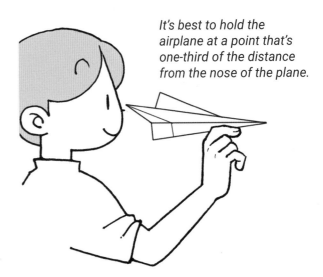

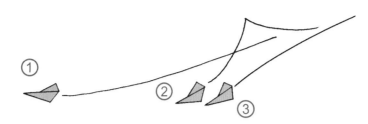

① If it flies straight and smoothly like in trajectory 1 above, it's ready—the elevators are angled correctly.

② If it quickly ascends and then dives like in trajectory 2, the angle of the elevators is too steep. Adjust by slightly lowering them.

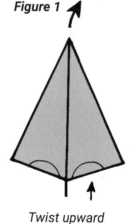

③ If it drops straight down like in trajectory 3, the angle of the elevators is too shallow. Adjust by slightly raising them.

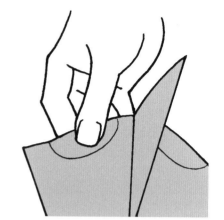

4 ▶ Adjustments for Left or Right Turns

If the airplane tends to curve left or right, adjust by tweaking only one of the elevators. Twisting the right elevator upward will make the airplane curve to the right (Figure 1). Twisting the left elevator upward will make it curve to the left.

   Also, looking at the vertical tail from above, twisting it to the right will make the airplane turn right (Figure 2), and twisting it to the left will make it turn left.

Figure 1

Twist upward

Figure 2

Twist to the right

Avoid touching the vertical tail if possible

Adjusting the vertical tail first can balance the flight, but it makes the airplane more vulnerable to destabilization from air current turbulence. It's better to adjust the direction by tweaking the elevators on the main wings whenever possible.

How to Throw an Airplane Hard (for Long Distance Flights)

Hold it naturally with a slight upward tilt and throw it straight ahead with all your might. The sequence of actions should be quick, and it's best if you release the airplane just before your hand is fully extended. Visualize throwing the paper airplane straight ahead—not high into the air.

A More Gentle Throwing Method (for Test Flights, Etc.)

This is a method of throwing suitable for when you are adjusting the paper airplane and confirming the effects of the adjustments with gentle test flights. Push the airplane straight out from beside your face. It's a gentle throw that's also suitable for young children, the elderly or anyone not able to execute the hard throw described above.

SPEAR PLANE

The shape of this plane resembles the tip of a spear. It's the simplest to fold, and the easiest to throw a great distance, so it's recommended for everyone from children to adults.

Type .... **Dart Series**
Paper Shape .. **Rectangular**
Difficulty .... ★

① Fold in half, and then unfold and flip over.

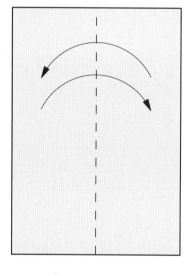

② Fold to the center crease.

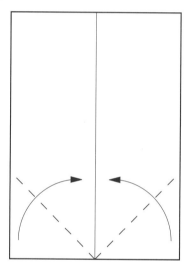

③ Fold to the center crease again.

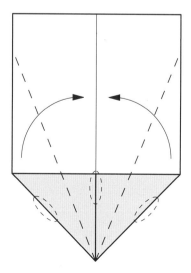

④ Make a pinch mark at the center, as indicated, and then unfold.

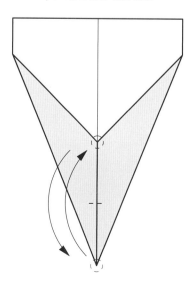

⑤ Fold the tip to the mark made in step 4.

⑥ Fold in half toward the back side.

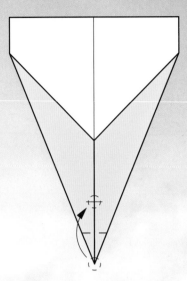

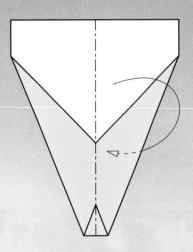

⑦ Fold the top layer down to meet the bottom edge. Do the same on the opposite side.

⑧ Open out the wings as shown in the 3D diagrams below. Complete.

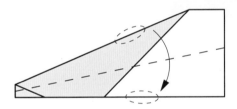

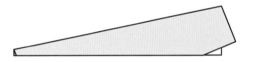

Check after folding ▶ Spear Plane 3D Views

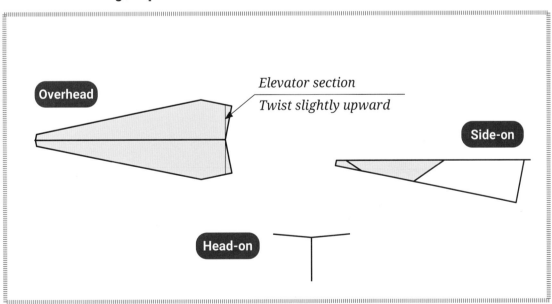

Overhead

Elevator section
Twist slightly upward

Side-on

Head-on

LANCER ZERO

Similar in shape to the Spear Plane (page 14) but designed with stronger wings to withstand powerful throws and fly greater distances.

Type .... **Dart Series**
Paper Shape .. **Rectangular**
Difficulty .... ★★

① Fold in half, and then unfold and flip over.

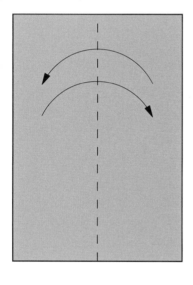

② Fold as indicated.

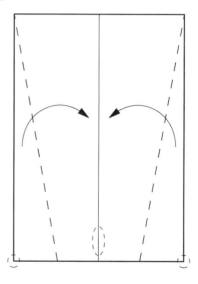

③ Fold to the center crease.

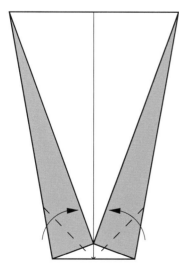

④ Fold the indicated edges to the center.

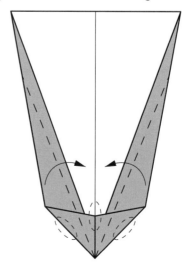

⑤ Fold at the position shown in the diagram.

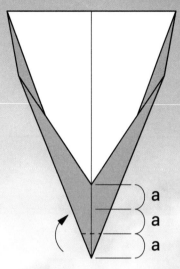

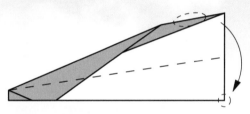

a
a
a

⑥ Fold in half toward the back side.

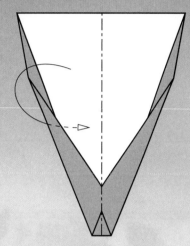

⑦ Fold the top layer down as indicated. Do the same on the opposite side.

⑧ Fold the top layer up as indicated. Do the same on the opposite side.

⑨ Open out the wings as shown in the 3D diagrams below. Complete.

Check after folding ▶ Lancer Zero 3D Views

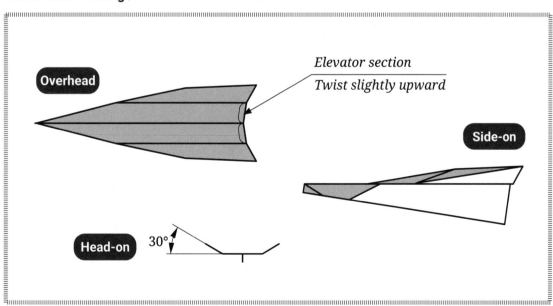

Overhead

Elevator section
Twist slightly upward

Side-on

Head-on   30°

SHOOTING FIGHTER

Adding a "cockpit" at the tip of the Spear Plane (page 14) acts as a stabilizer that prevents this plane from swaying from side to side and enables it to fly farther.

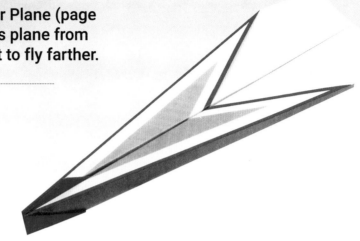

Type .... **Dart Series**

Paper Shape .. **Rectangular**

Difficulty .... ★★

① Fold in half, and then unfold and flip over.

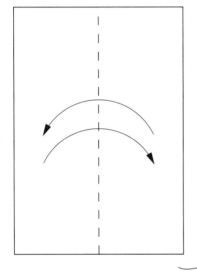

② Fold to the center crease, and then flip over.

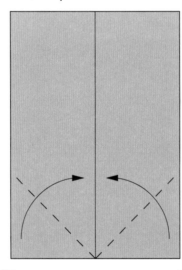

③ Fold to the center crease.

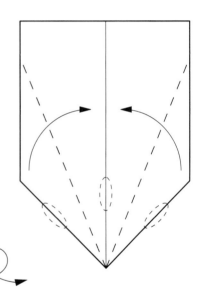

④ Swing the flaps out from behind.

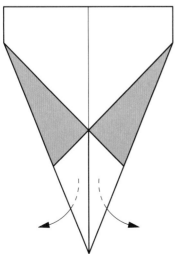

⑤ Fold as indicated.

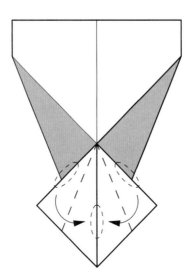

⑥ Form a crease between the indicated points.

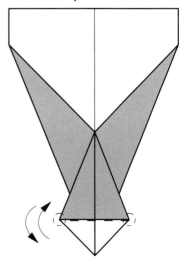

⑦ Fold as indicated, and then flip over.

⑧ Fold along the crease made in step 6.

⑨ Fold in half toward the back side.

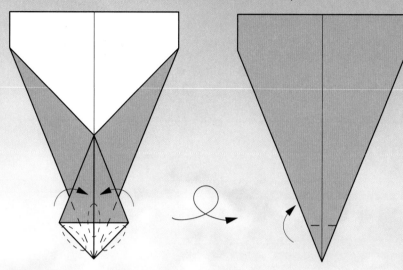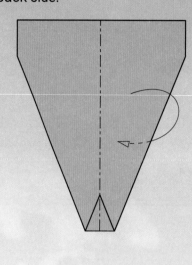

⑩ Fold the top layer as indicated. Do the same on the opposite side.

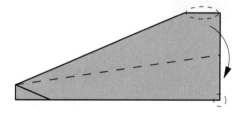

⑪ Open out the wings as shown in the 3D diagrams below. Complete.

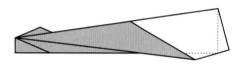

Check after folding ▶ Shooting Fighter 3D Views

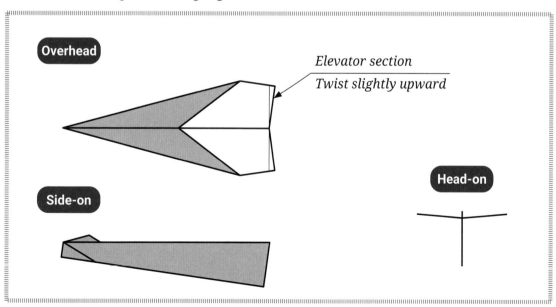

Overhead

Elevator section
Twist slightly upward

Side-on

Head-on

ARROW FIGHTER

With its barbed nose, this dart is reminiscent of an arrow streaking toward its mark. The arrowhead part involves many folds, so fold precisely.

Type .... **Dart Series**
Paper Shape .. **Rectangular**
Difficulty .... ★★★

① Fold vertically and horizontally in half, and then unfold and flip over.

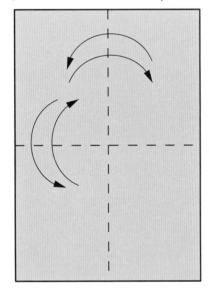

② Fold the bottom edge to the center horizontal crease, and then unfold.

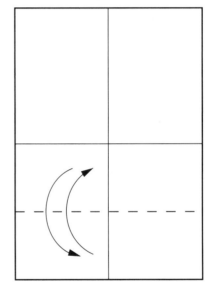

③ Fold the edge to the crease made in step 2.

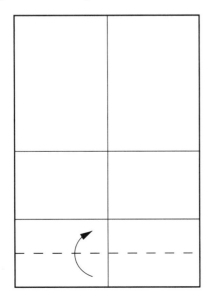

④ Fold between the indicated points.

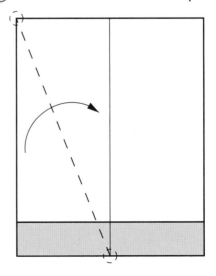

⑤ Fold between the indicated points. Unfold.

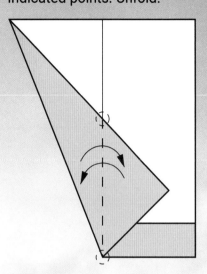

⑥ Fold as indicated.

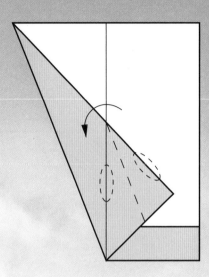

⑦ Fold between the indicated points. Unfold.

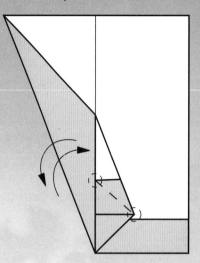

⑧ Lift the top layer and fold it so that the step-7 crease becomes a mountain fold.

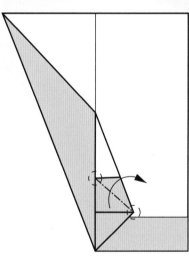

⑨ Fold between the indicated points.

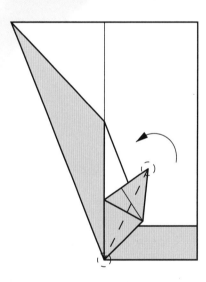

⑩ Fold along the crease made in step 5.

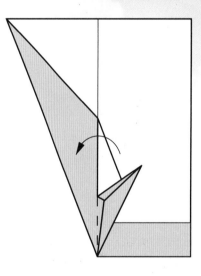

⑪ Swing open the flap while preserving the step-10 fold.

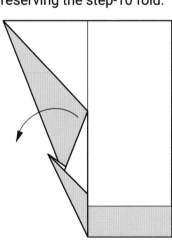

⑫ Fold the opposite side in the same way as steps 4–11.

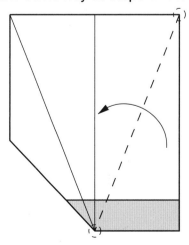

⑬ Fold as indicated.

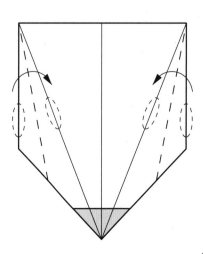

⑭ Fold along the creases made in steps 4 and 12.

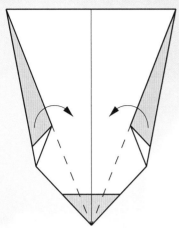

⑮ Fold between the indicated points.

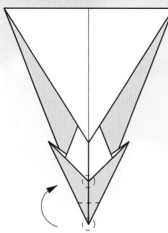

⑯ Fold in half toward the back side.

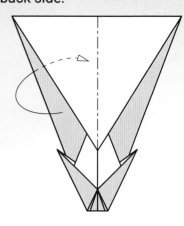

⑰ Fold as indicated, and then unfold.

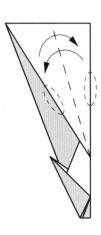

⑱ Inside-reverse fold along the crease from step 17. Refer to page 8.

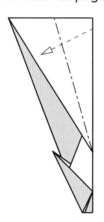

⑲ Fold the top layer between the indicated points. Fold the opposite side in the same way.

a a

⑳ Open out the wings as shown in the 3D diagrams at right. Complete.

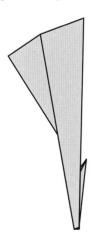

Check after folding ▶ Arrow Fighter 3D Views

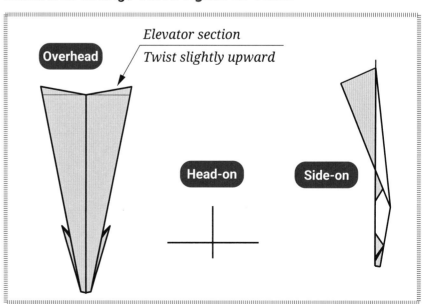

Overhead

Elevator section
Twist slightly upward

Head-on

Side-on

LANCER

The term "lancer" refers to a cavalryman armed with a long spear. This model was designed for distance competitions, inspired by the powerful image of a hurtling spear. It uses a unique folding method that is asymmetrically diagonal.

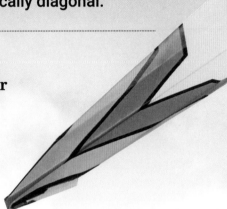

Type .... **Dart Series**
Paper Shape .. **Rectangular**
Difficulty .... ★★★★

① Fold in half, and then unfold.

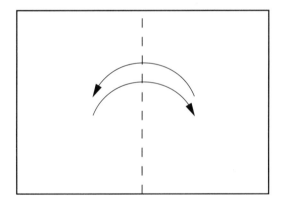

② Fold as indicated, and then unfold.

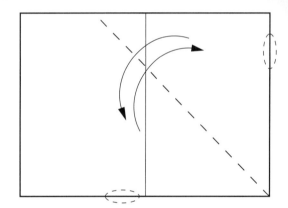

③ Fold as indicated, and then unfold.

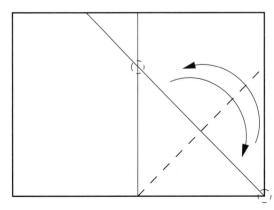

④ Fold as indicated.

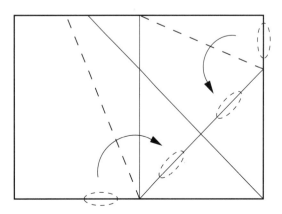

⑤ Fold in half and flip over.

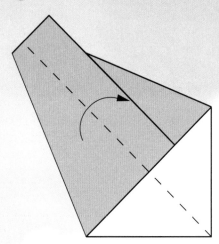

⑥ Fold as indicated.

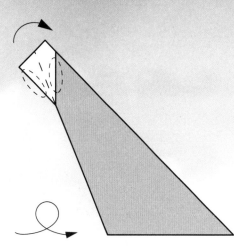

⑦ Unfold.

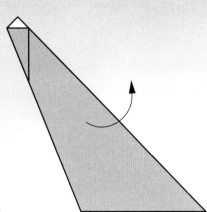

⑧ Fold as indicated, and then unfold.

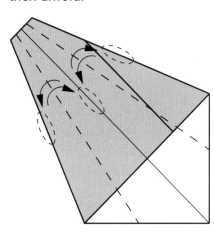

⑨ Fold to meet the creases from step 8.

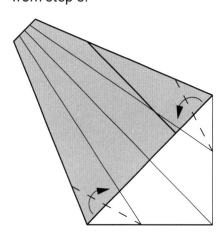

⑩ Fold again to meet the creases from step 8.

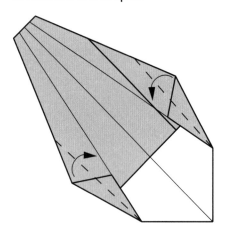

⑪ Fold along the creases from step 8.

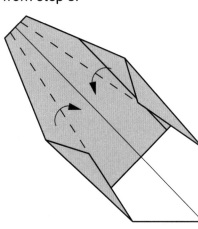

⑫ Fold inside.

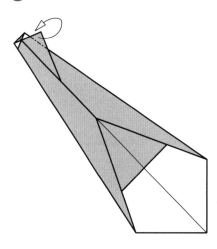

⑬ Fold in half toward the back.

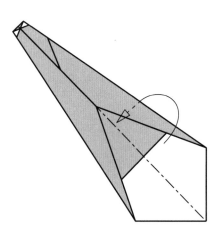

⑭ Fold the top layer at the position shown in the diagram. Fold the opposite side in the same way.

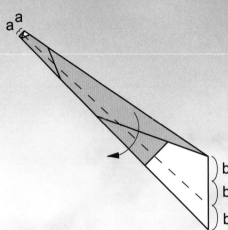

⑮ Fold at the mark, and then unfold. Fold the opposite side similarly, and open back to the state of step 13.

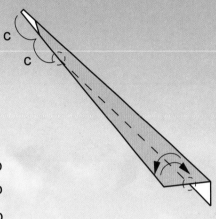

⑯ Fold as indicated.

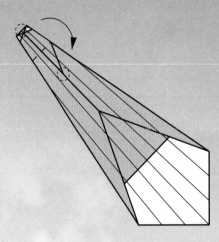

⑰ Fold at the mark, unfold, and then inside-reverse fold. Refer to page 8.

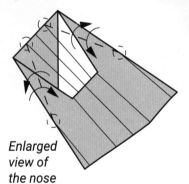

Enlarged view of the nose

⑱ Fold in half toward the back side.

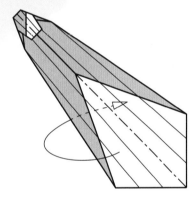

⑲ Open out the wings as shown in the 3D diagrams below. Complete.

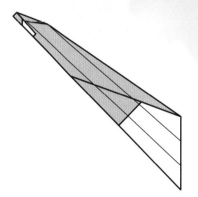

Check after folding ▶ Lancer 3D Views

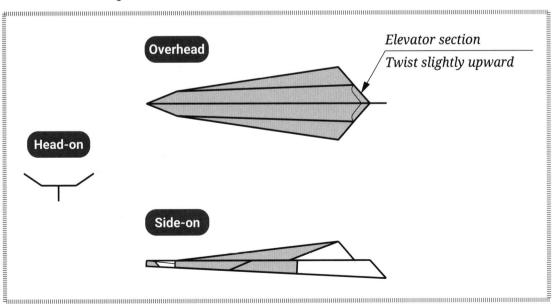

Overhead

Elevator section
Twist slightly upward

Head-on

Side-on

SKY JET

This is an evolved version of the Shooting Fighter (page 18). The wings have been reinforced to withstand strong throws, allowing it to fly farther.

Type .... **Dart Series**

Paper Shape .. **Rectangular**

Difficulty .... ★★

① Fold in half and unfold, and then fold between the indicated points.

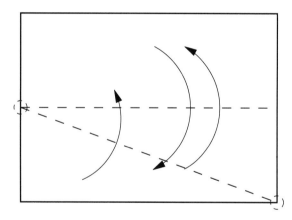

② Fold between the indicated points.

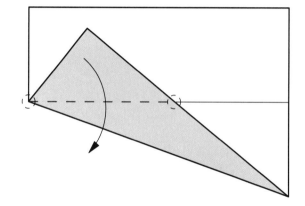

③ Fold the opposite side in the same way as steps 1 and 2.

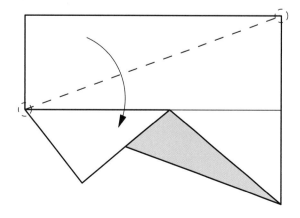

④ Swing the flaps open toward the back.

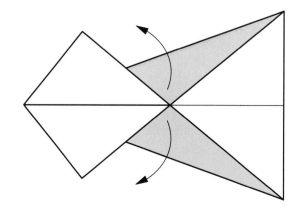

⑤ Fold as indicated.

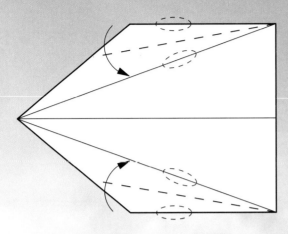

⑥ Fold along the creases from steps 1 and 3.

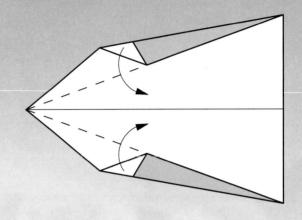

⑦ Swing the flaps around from the back.

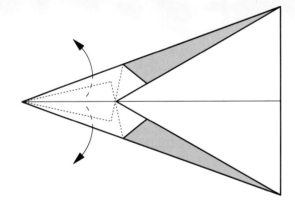

⑧ Fold as indicated.

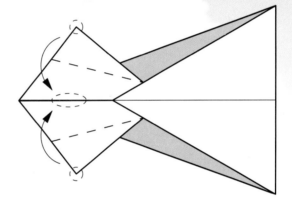

⑨ Fold as indicated, and then flip over.

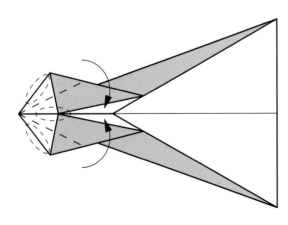

⑩ Fold as indicated, and then fold in half toward the back side.

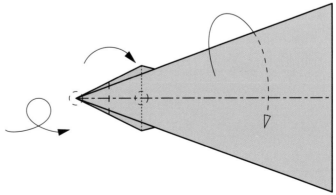

⑪ Fold as indicated.

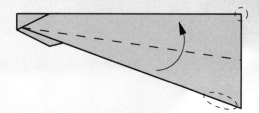

⑫ Fold the opposite side in the same way.

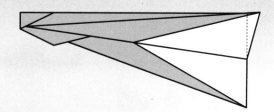

⑬ Open out the wings as shown in the 3D diagrams below. Complete.

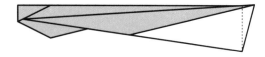

Check after folding ▶ Sky Jet 3D Views

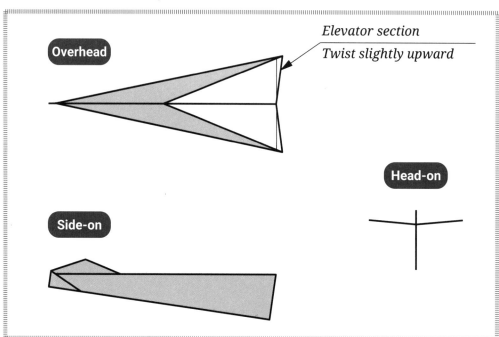

Overhead

Elevator section
Twist slightly upward

Head-on

Side-on

SQUID AIRPLANE

This model represents one of the traditional paper airplane folding methods, characterized by its squid-like shape. It's an easy-to-fold airplane with good balance—and it's easy to fly!

Type .... **Squid Series**

Paper Shape .. **Rectangular**

Difficulty .... ★

① Fold in half, and then unfold. Fold the left corner flaps to the center crease and flip over.

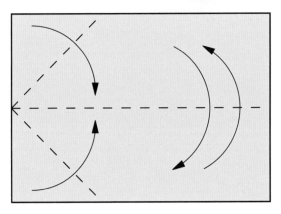

② Fold to the center crease.

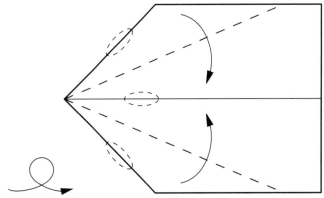

③ Swing the flaps out from behind.

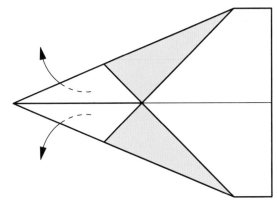

④ Fold as indicated.

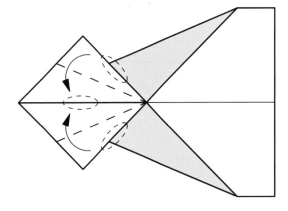

⑤ Fold between the circled points.

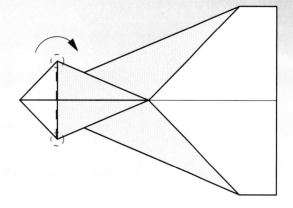

⑥ Fold in half toward the back side.

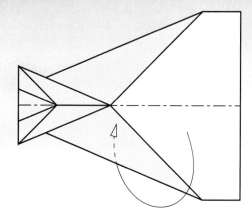

⑦ Fold the top layer as indicated. Fold the opposite side in the same way.

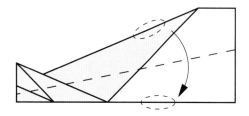

⑧ Open out the wings as shown in the 3D diagrams below. Complete.

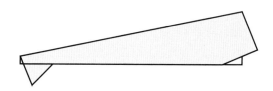

Check after folding ▶ Squid Airplane 3D Views

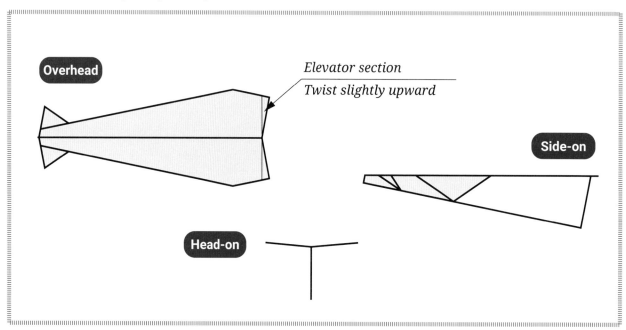

Overhead

Elevator section
Twist slightly upward

Side-on

Head-on

SQUID AIRPLANE S

I have improved upon the Squid Airplane (page 29) by making the fins smaller, streamlining it like a darting squid, enhancing its flight performance.

Type .... **Squid Series**
Paper Shape .. **Rectangular**
Difficulty .... ★★

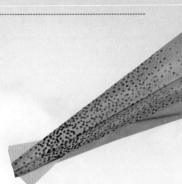

① Fold in half, and then unfold. Fold the left corner flaps to the center crease and flip over.

② Fold to the center crease.

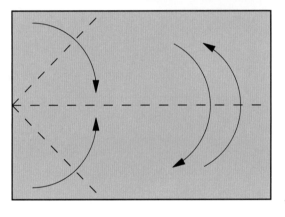

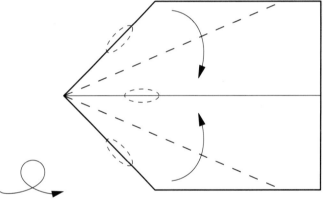

③ Swing the flaps out from behind.

④ Fold as indicated.

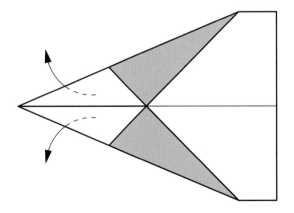

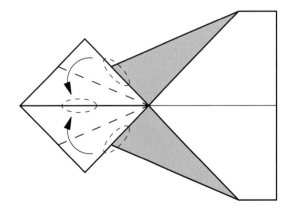

⑤ Fold as indicated.

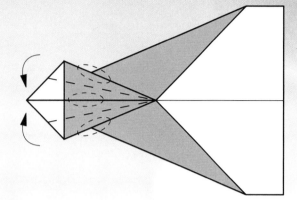

⑥ Fold between the circled points.

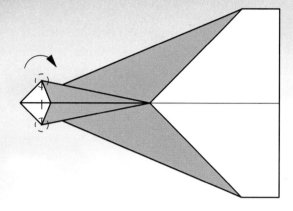

⑦ Fold in half toward the back side.

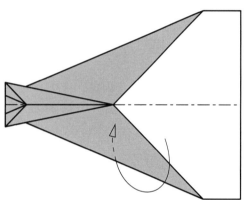

⑧ Fold the top layer as indicated. Fold the opposite side in the same way.

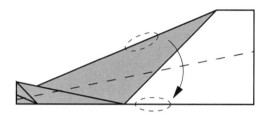

⑨ Open out the wings as shown in the 3D diagrams below. Complete.

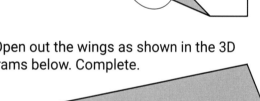

Check after folding ▶ Squid Airplane S 3D Views

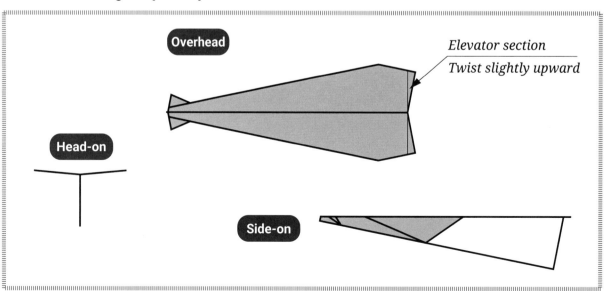

Overhead

Elevator section
Twist slightly upward

Head-on

Side-on

PRAYING MANTIS

This plane's rear-swept forewings resemble the folded grasping legs of a praying mantis. This variation of the Squid Airplane (page 29) is very stable in flight.

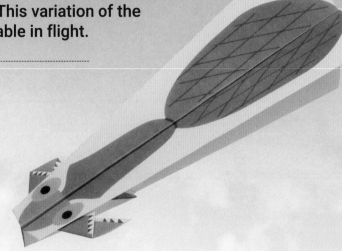

Type .... **Squid Series**

Paper Shape .. **Rectangular**

Difficulty .... ★★

① Fold in half, and then unfold. Fold the left corner flaps to the center crease and flip over.

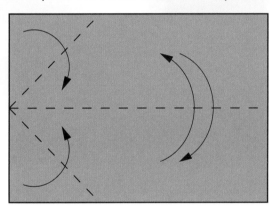

② Fold to the center crease.

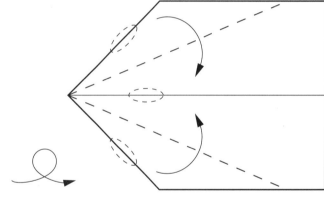

③ Swing the flaps out from behind.

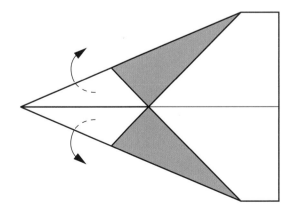

④ Fold as indicated.

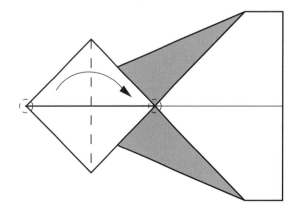

⑤ Fold as indicated, with the creases beginning at the center horizontal crease, under the flaps.

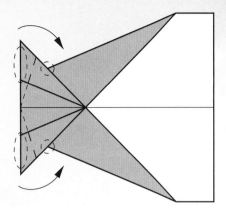

⑥ Fold in half toward the back side.

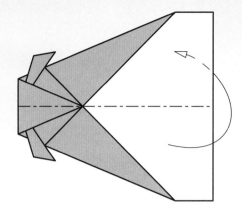

⑦ Fold the top layer as indicated. Fold the opposite side in the same way.

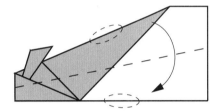

⑧ Open out the wings as shown in the 3D diagrams below. Complete.

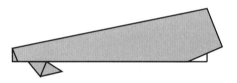

Check after folding ▶ Praying Mantis 3D Views

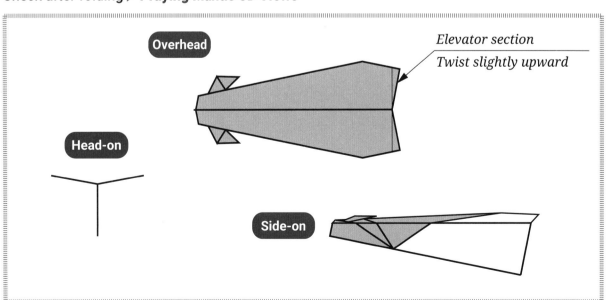

SOLEIL

This model looks cool and is very easy to fold, but it has large expanses of thin wing surface, making it a challenge to fly straight.

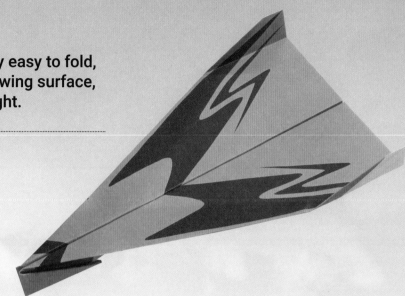

Type .... **Jet Series**
Paper Shape .. **Rectangular**
Difficulty .... ★★

① Fold vertically and horizontally in half, and then unfold and flip over.

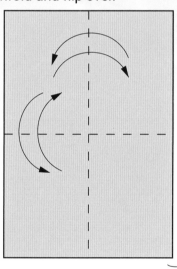

② Fold the bottom edge to the center horizontal crease, and then unfold.

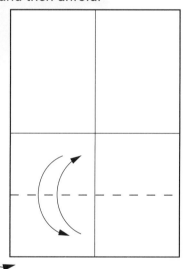

③ Fold the edge to the crease made in step 2.

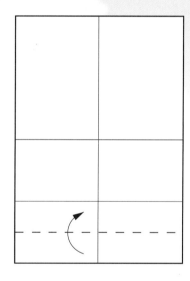

④ Fold the bottom corner flaps to the center vertical crease.

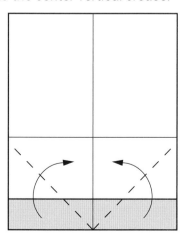

⑤ Fold to the center crease and unfold.

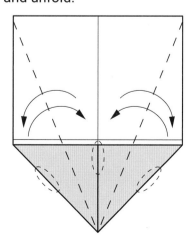

⑥ Fold the sides to the creases made in step 5.

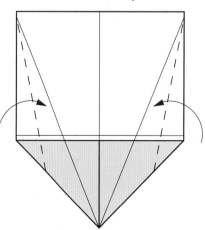

⑦ Fold in on the creases made in step 5.

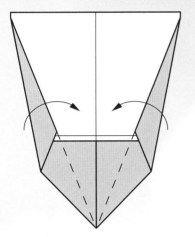

⑧ Fold as indicated.

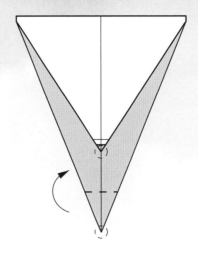

⑨ Fold in half toward the back side.

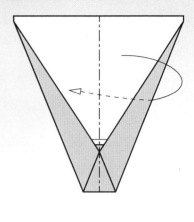

⑩ Fold the top layer to the width of "a." Fold the opposite side in the same way.

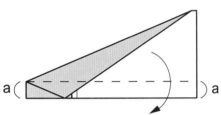

⑪ Fold the top layer to the width of "a." Fold the opposite side in the same way.

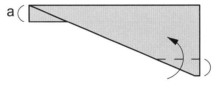

⑫ Open out the wings as shown in the 3D diagrams below. Complete.

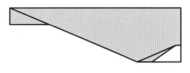

Check after folding ▶ Soleil 3D Views

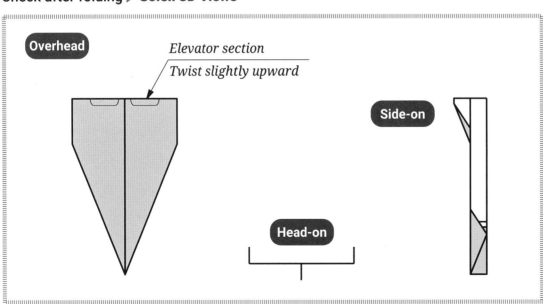

Overhead

Elevator section
Twist slightly upward

Side-on

Head-on

CONCORDE

This airplane is folded from a square piece of paper and was inspired by the famous supersonic Concorde airliner from France and the United Kingdom.

Type .... **Jet Series**
Paper Shape .. **Square**
Difficulty .... ★★★

① Fold corner to corner both ways, unfolding after each. Fold the bottom corner to the center.

② Fold as indicated.

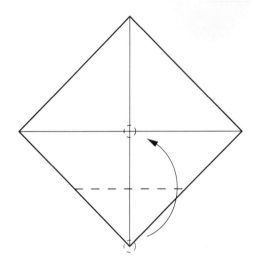

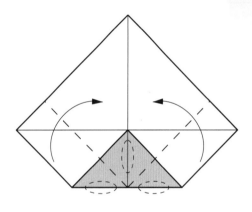

③ Fold the lower edges to the center crease, and then unfold.

④ Fold parts of the upper edges to the creases from step 3.

⑤ Fold again to the creases from step 3.

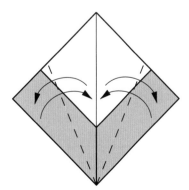

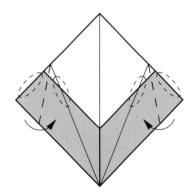

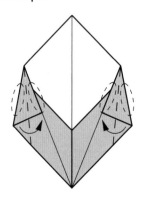

⑥ Fold in along the creases from step 3.

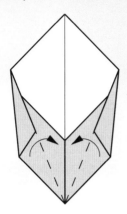

⑦ Fold in half toward the back side.

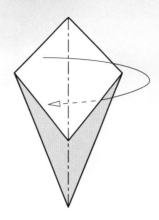

⑧ Fold between the indicated points and then unfold. Inside-reverse fold along the crease. Refer to page 8.

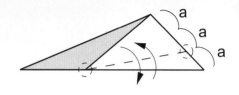

⑨ Fold the top layer between the indicated points. Fold the opposite side in the same way.

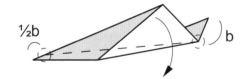

⑩ Open out the wings as shown in the 3D diagrams below. Complete.

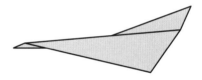

Check after folding ▶ Concorde 3D Views

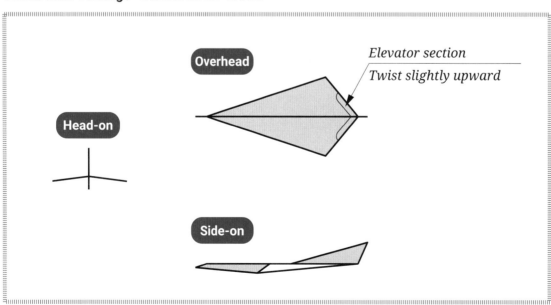

BOMBER

In this airplane design, the usual fuselage part acts as an auxiliary "lifting body" wing, and the part resembling a tail fin becomes the main wing.

Type .... **Jet Series**
Paper Shape .. **Square**
Difficulty .... ★★★★

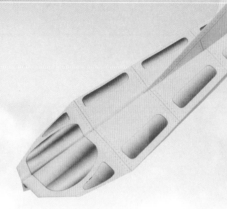

① Fold in half vertically and diagonally both ways, unfolding after each. Then, flip over.

② Fold as indicated.

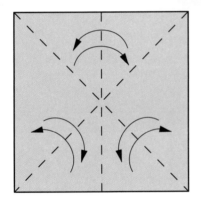

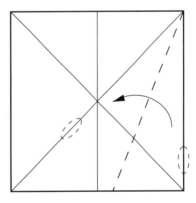

③ Fold between the circled points.

④ Fold the flap from step 3 inside. Fold the opposite side in the same way as steps 2–4.

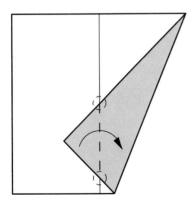

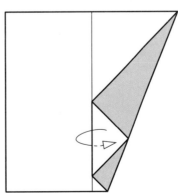

⑤ Fold as indicated, and then unfold.

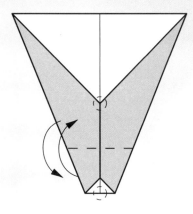

⑥ Fold between the indicated points.

a

a

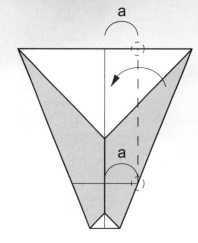

⑦ Fold between the indicated points, and then unfold to the state of step 5.

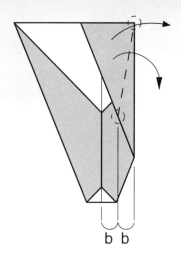

b b

⑧ Double inside-reverse fold along the creases from steps 6 and 7. Refer to page 8.

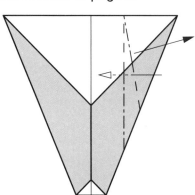

⑨ Fold the opposite side in the same way as steps 6–8.

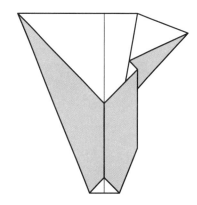

⑩ Fold inside at 4 locations as indicated.

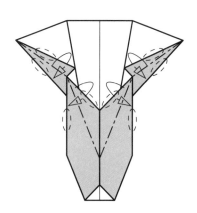

⑪ Fold to the center crease.

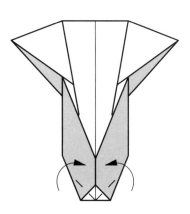

⑫ Fold as indicated.

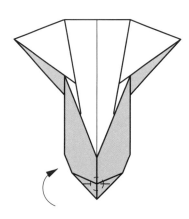

⑬ Fold in half toward the back side.

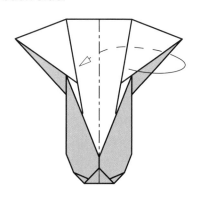

⑭ Fold between the indicated points, and then unfold.

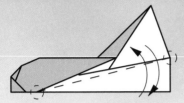

⑮ Inside-reverse fold along the crease from step 14. Refer to page 8.

⑯ Fold the top layer between the indicated points. Fold the opposite side in the same way.

c
2c

⑰ Open out the wings as shown in the 3D diagrams below. Complete.

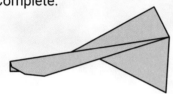

Check after folding ▶ Bomber 3D Views

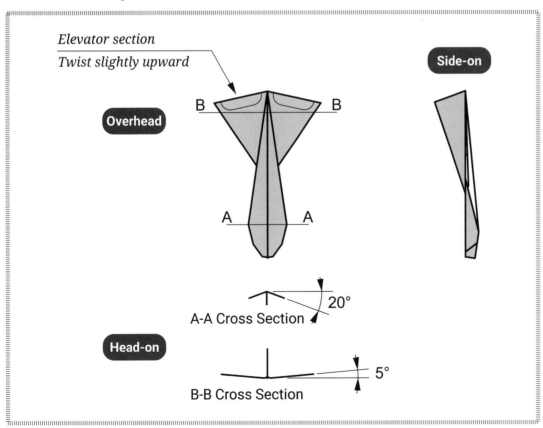

Elevator section
Twist slightly upward

B   B

Overhead

A   A

Side-on

20°
A-A Cross Section

Head-on

5°
B-B Cross Section

SHARK

This airplane looks like a sawshark from the side, making it a distinctive and cool design. It's the first in this book to feature a double inside-reverse folded vertical stabilizer.

Type .... **Jet Series**
Paper Shape .. **Square**
Difficulty .... ★★★★★

① Fold in half corner to corner, and then unfold.
② Fold the bottom edges to the center crease, and then unfold.

③ Fold the indicated portions of the top edges to the creases made in step 2.

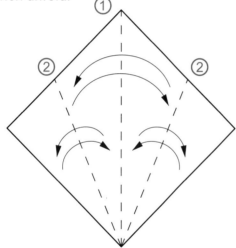

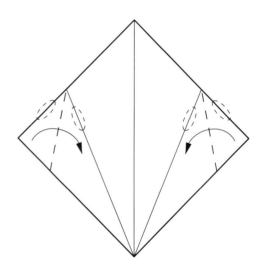

④ Fold in along the existing step-2 creases, and then flip over.

⑤ Fold as indicated, and then flip over.

⑥ Fold as indicated, and then flip over.

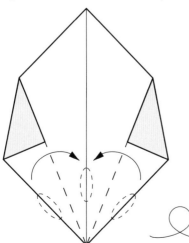

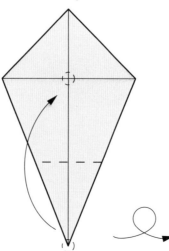

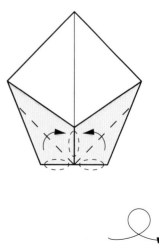

⑦ Pull open a pocket on both sides, pivoting the flap downward as you flatten it.

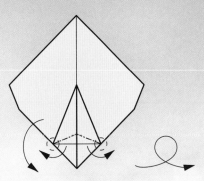

⑧ Fold both sides between the indicated points. Then, flip over.

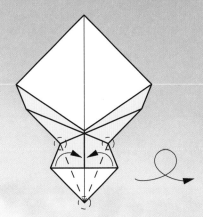

⑨ Fold as indicated, and then flip over.

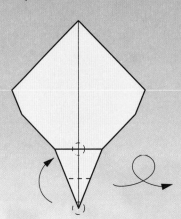

⑩ Fold both sides to the center crease. Then, flip over.

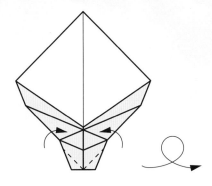

⑪ As in step 7, pull open a pocket on both sides, pivoting the flap downward as you flatten it. Then, flip over.

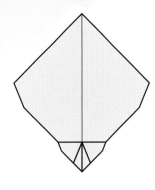
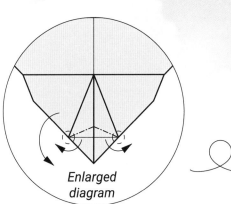

Enlarged diagram

⑫ Fold as indicated, and then fold the entire paper in half.

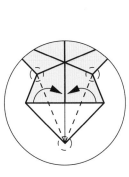

Enlarged diagram

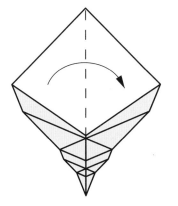

⑬ Fold as indicated.

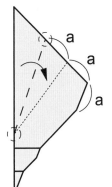

a
a
a

⑭ Fold the top layer as indicated, and then unfold steps 13–14.

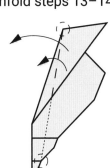

⑮ Double inside-reverse fold along the creases from steps 13–14. Refer to page 8.

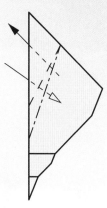

⑯ Fold the top layer between the indicted points, and then unfold.

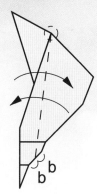

⑰ Refold step 16, but this time leave section "c" in place.

⑱ Fold the section "c" along the crease from step 16.

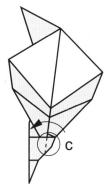

⑲ Fold between the indicated points. Fold the opposite side in the same way as steps 16–19.

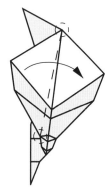

⑳ Open out the wings as shown in the 3D diagrams below. Complete.

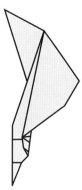

Check after folding ▶ Shark 3D Views

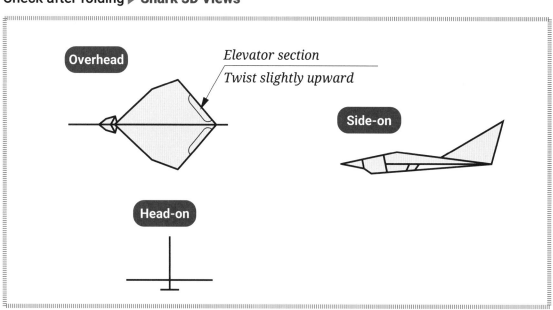

GHOST 3.0

Further improvements to its predecessor have resulted in this advanced model. With its center of gravity shifted forward, this plane flies smoothly and maintains good balance.

Type .... Jet Series

Paper Shape .. Rectangular

Difficulty .... ★★★★

① Fold in half, and then unfold. Then, fold the bottom corner flaps to the center vertical crease.

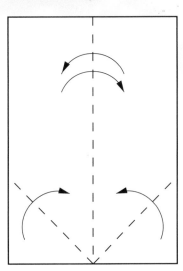

② Fold to the center crease, and then flip over.

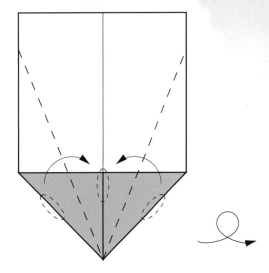

③ Fold as indicated, and then flip over.

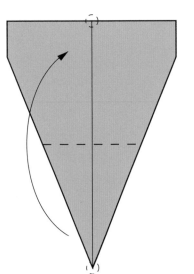

④ Fold as indicated, and then flip over.

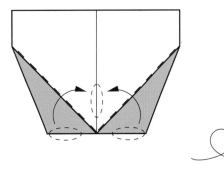

⑤ Fold as indicated. Then, flip over.

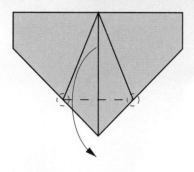

⑥ Fold the top layer as indicated.

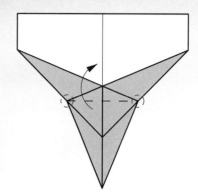

⑦ Fold pockets to the left and right, and then flatten.

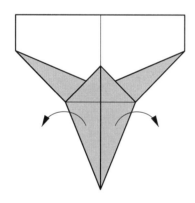

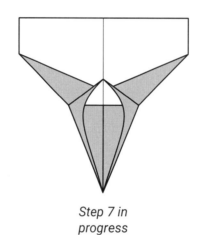

Step 7 in progress

⑧ Fold as indicated.

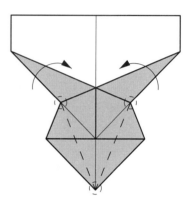

⑨ Fold as indicated.

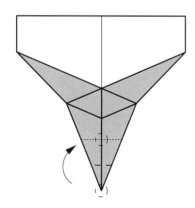

⑩ Fold in half toward the back side.

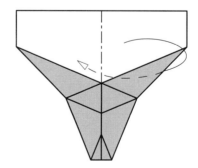

⑪ Fold at the indicated position, and then unfold. Inside-reverse fold. Refer to page 8.

⑫ Fold the top layer between the indicted points. Fold the opposite side in the same way.

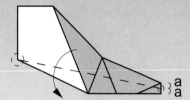

⑬ Fold the top layer between the indicted points. Fold the opposite side in the same way.

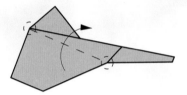

⑭ Open out the wings as shown in the 3D diagrams below. Complete.

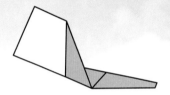

Check after folding ▶ Ghost 3.0 3D Views

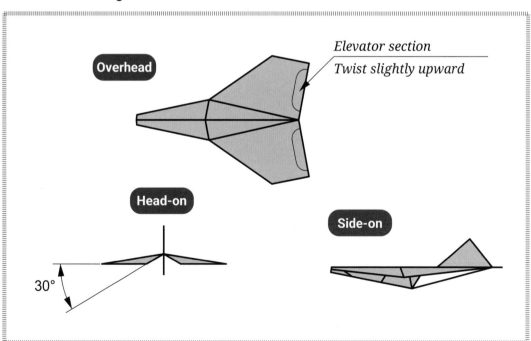

Overhead

Elevator section
Twist slightly upward

Head-on

30°

Side-on

FULLBACK

Inspired by a tailless fighter jet, this model features a sleek, cool-looking fuselage.

Type .... **Jet Series**

Paper Shape .. **Rectangular**

Difficulty .... ★★★★

① Fold in half, and then unfold and flip over.

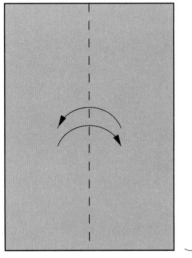

② Fold the corner flaps to the center crease.

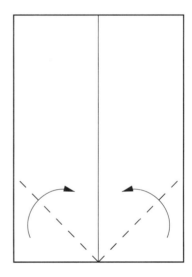

③ Fold as indicated.

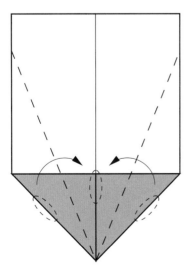

④ Fold bottom to top, and then flip over.

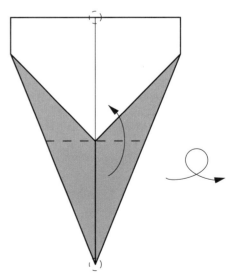

⑤ Fold at the indicated position.

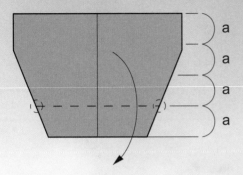

a
a
a
a

⑥ While folding down the "b" flaps as indicated, also fold in the underlying "c" edges, which will be pulled into position.

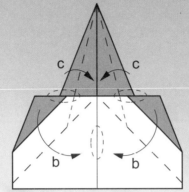

c   c

b   b

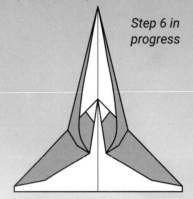

Step 6 in progress

⑦ Fold as indicated.

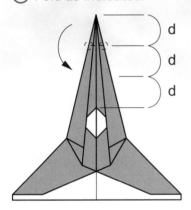

d
d
d

⑧ Fold in half toward the back side.

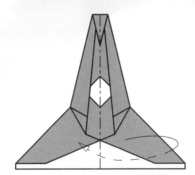

⑨ Fold the top layer at the indicated position. Fold the opposite side in the same way.

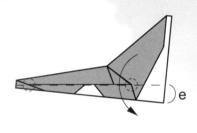

e

⑩ Fold the top layer to the width of "e" from step 9. Fold the opposite side in the same way. Open out the wings as shown in the 3D diagrams at right. Complete.

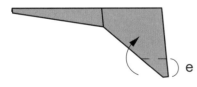

e

Check after folding ▶ Fullback 3D Views

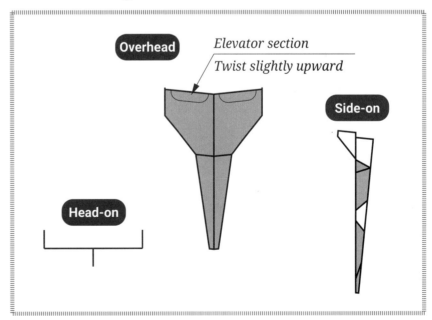

Overhead

Elevator section

Twist slightly upward

Side-on

Head-on

FIRE X

This plane is similar to the Fullback (page 48) in folding method, but with added forward wings, the need to manipulate the elevator is minimized, enhancing stability.

Type .... **Jet Series**
Paper Shape .. **Rectangular**
Difficulty .... ★★★★★

① Fold in half, and then unfold. Then, fold the bottom corner flaps to the center vertical crease.

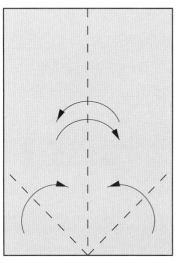

② Fold as indicated.

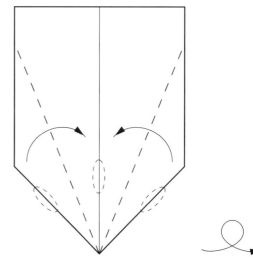

③ Fold bottom to top, and then flip over.

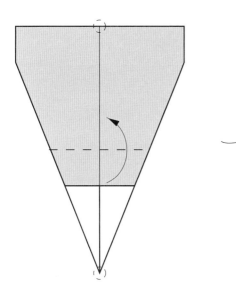

④ Fold and unfold as indicated, and then flip over.

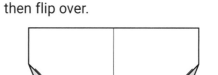
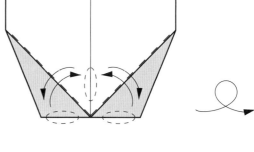

⑤ Fold and unfold as indicated.

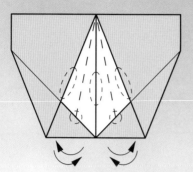

⑥ Fold the flap down at the indicated position.

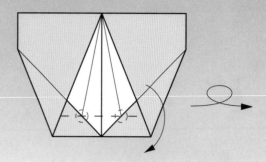

⑦ While refolding along the creases from step 4, also fold in the underlying edges, which will be pulled into position.

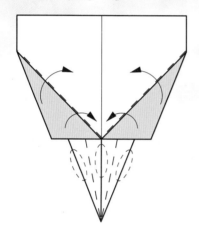

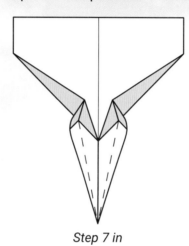

Step 7 in progress

⑧ Swing out the underlying flaps.

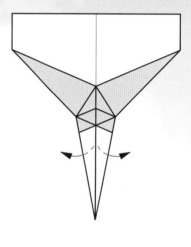

⑨ Fold as indicated.

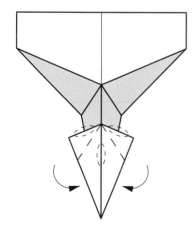

⑩ Fold between the indicated points.

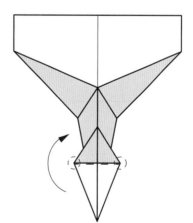

⑪ Fold in half toward the back side.

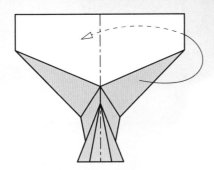

⑫ Fold the top layer between the indicated points. Fold the opposite side in the same way.

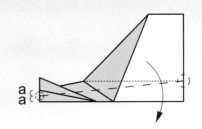

⑬ Parallel to the crease from step 12, fold the top layer as indicated. Fold the opposite side in the same way. Open out the wings as shown in the 3D diagrams below. Complete.

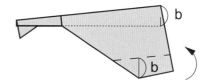

Check after folding ▶ Fire X 3D Views

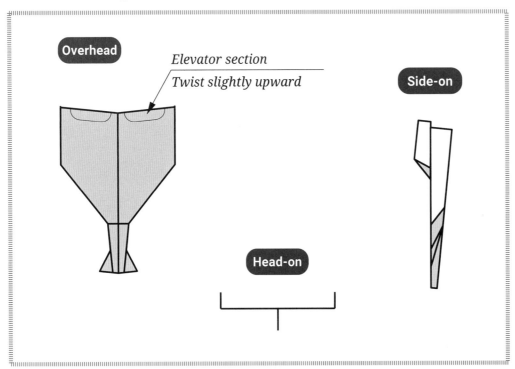

Overhead

Elevator section
Twist slightly upward

Side-on

Head-on

SHOOTER

Its smooth, straight flight resembles an otter gliding through water.

Type .... **Jet Series**
Paper Shape .. **Square**
Difficulty .... ★★★★★

① Fold in half in four directions (vertically, horizontally, and diagonally both ways), unfolding after each.

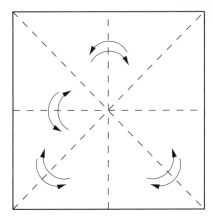

② Fold as indicated.

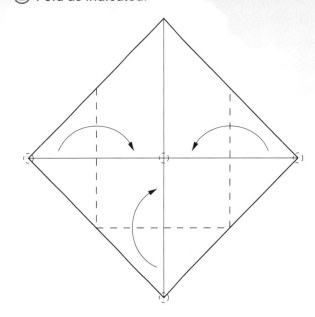

③ Fold as indicated.

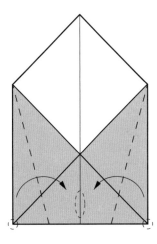

④ Fold as indicated.

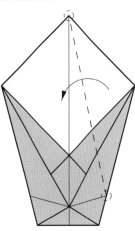

⑤ Fold between the indicated points, and then open.

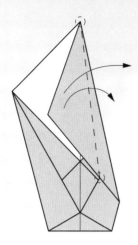

⑥ Make a double inside-reverse fold along the creases from steps 4 and 5. Refer to page 8.

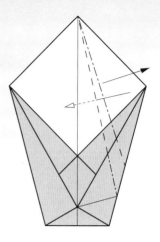

⑦ Pivot the flap downward.

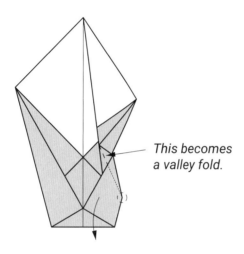

This becomes a valley fold.

⑧ Fold the opposite side in the same way as steps 4–7.

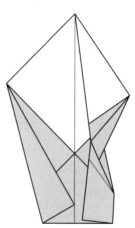

⑨ Fold as indicated.

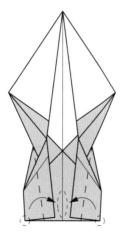

⑩ Fold to the vertical crease.

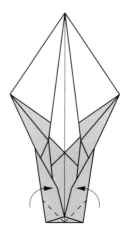

⑪ Fold at the indicated position.

⑫ Fold in half toward the back side.

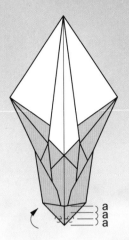

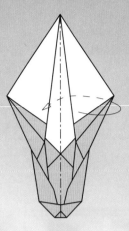

⑬ Fold at the indicated position, and then unfold and inside-reverse fold. Refer to page 8.

⑭ Fold the top layer between the indicated points. Fold the opposite side in the same way.

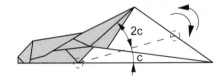

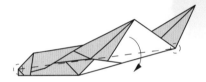

⑮ Open out the wings as shown in the 3D diagrams below. Complete.

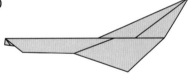

Check after folding ▶ Shooter 3D Views

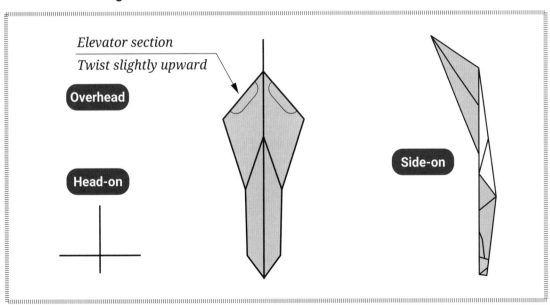

Elevator section
Twist slightly upward

Overhead

Head-on

Side-on

LONG PLANE

At first glance, it appears simple, but this airplane is surprisingly challenging to fold. If the wings are relatively untwisted, it will fly beautifully straight.

Type .... **Belly-button Series**
Paper Shape .. **Rectangular**
Difficulty .... ★★★

① Fold in half vertically, and then unfold.
② Fold in half horizontally.

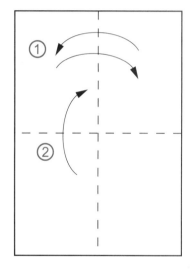

③ Fold in half again, and then open up completely.

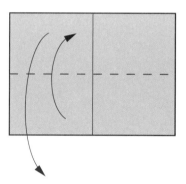

④ Fold as indicated.

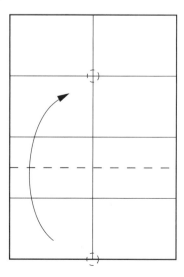

⑤ Fold as indicated.

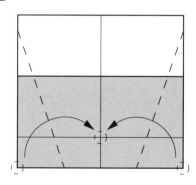

⑥ Fold as indicated.

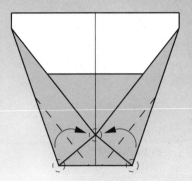

⑦ Fold as indicated.

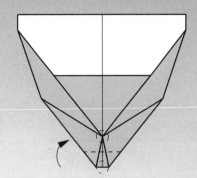

⑧ Fold in half toward the back side.

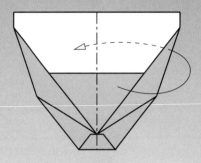

⑨ Fold as indicated, and then unfold.

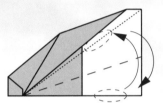

⑩ Inside-reverse fold along the crease from step 9. Refer to page 8.

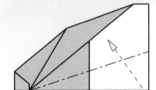

⑪ Fold the top layer at the indicated position. Fold the opposite side in the same way.

⑫ Open out the wings as shown in the 3D diagrams below. Complete.

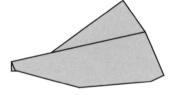

Check after folding ▶ Long Plane 3D Views

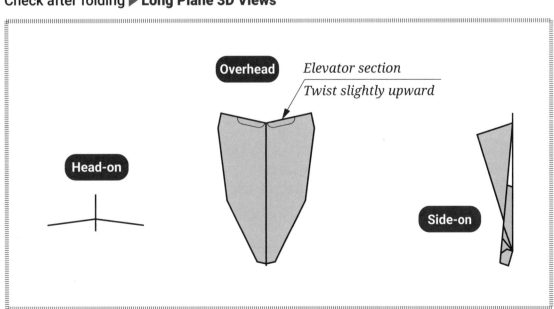

Head-on

Overhead

Elevator section

Twist slightly upward

Side-on

SUPER PLANE

The folding process up to a certain point is the same as for the Long Plane (page 56). The nose lock prevents the body from opening, reducing air resistance.

Type .... **Belly-button Series**
Paper Shape .. **Rectangular**
Difficulty .... ★★★

① Fold in half vertically, and then unfold.
② Fold in half horizontally.

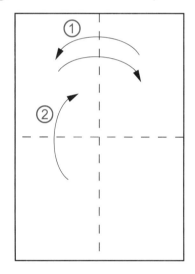

③ Fold in half again, and then open up completely.

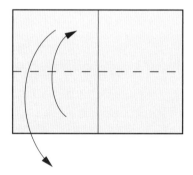

④ Fold as indicated.

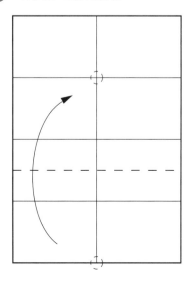

⑤ Fold as indicated.

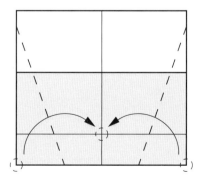

⑥ Fold as indicated.

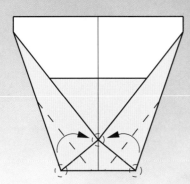

⑦ Fold as indicated, and then unfold.

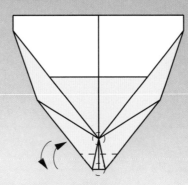

⑧ Fold in half toward the back side.

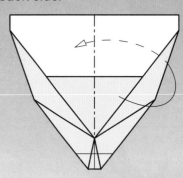

⑨ Fold the nose. Refer to the enlarged diagrams below.

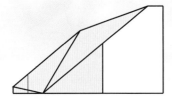

⑩ Fold the top layer as indicated. Fold the opposite side in the same way.

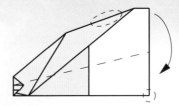

⑪ Open out the wings as shown in the 3D diagrams at the bottom. Complete.

Zoomed-in Diagrams: How to Fold the Nose

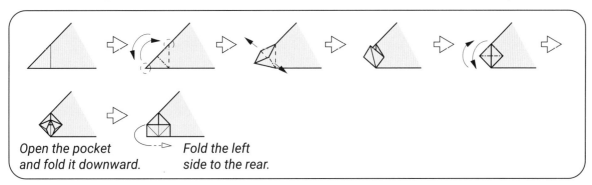

Open the pocket and fold it downward.   Fold the left side to the rear.

Check after folding ▶ Super Plane 3D Views

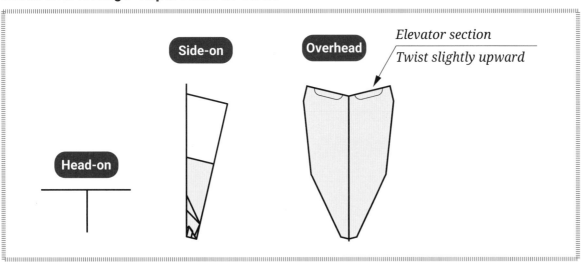

Side-on

Overhead

Elevator section
Twist slightly upward

Head-on

AIR KING

This airplane holds the Japanese record for distance competition (nearly 203 feet—61.82 meters). It's a new type that improves on the basic belly-button airplane by enhancing the wings' strength to withstand strong throws and provide better gliding performance.

Type .... **Belly-button Series**
Paper Shape .. **Rectangular**
Difficulty .... ★★★

① Fold in half, and then unfold and flip over.

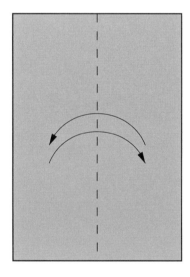

② Fold the corner flaps to the center crease.

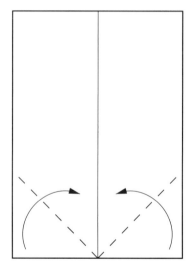

③ Fold as indicated.

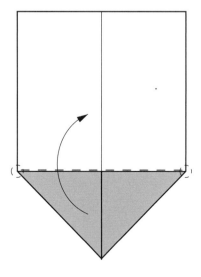

④ Fold as indicated, and then unfold.

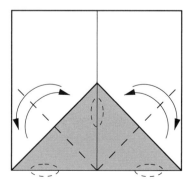

⑤ Fold as indicated, and then unfold.

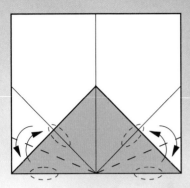

⑥ Fold as indicated.

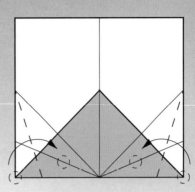

⑦ Fold along the creases from step 4.

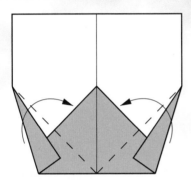

⑧ Fold between the indicated points.

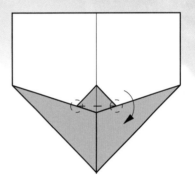

⑨ Fold to half the width of "a," and then unfold.

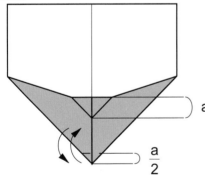

⑩ Fold in half toward the back side.

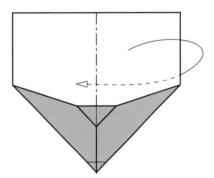

⑪ Fold the nose. Refer to the enlarged diagrams on page 62.

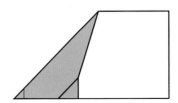

Zoomed-in Diagrams: How to Fold the Nose

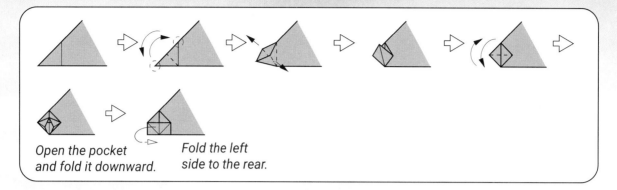

Open the pocket and fold it downward.

Fold the left side to the rear.

⑫ Fold the top layer as indicated. Fold the opposite side in the same way.

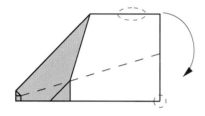

⑬ Open out the wings as shown in the 3D diagrams below. Complete.

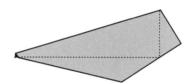

Check after folding ▶ Air King 3D Views

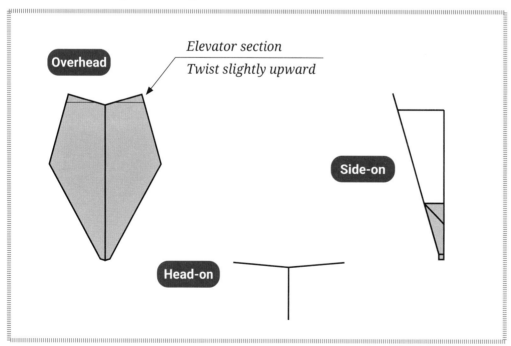

Overhead

Elevator section
Twist slightly upward

Side-on

Head-on

Origami Airplane Association

Established in 1995 following the publication of *Fly, Paper Airplane*, it now has an official competition rules set, hosts competitions and workshops based on those rules, and conducts lectures.
Website: http://www.oriplane.com/

Paper Airplane Museum

Opened on March 10, 2001, next to the owner's home, it is Japan's only museum dedicated to paper airplanes. It's a two-story building where the first floor displays hundreds of homemade origami airplanes and original works from paper airplane creators nationwide, and visitors can view videos in the video corner. The second floor has a large open space for origami airplane workshops, equipped with a wind tunnel experiment device to simulate the effects of wind on wings and the mechanics of lift. The walls display over 200 origami airplanes and works from paper airplane creators like Andrew Dewar and Yasuaki Ninomiya. Instructors are available when the museum is open, so paper airplane enthusiasts visiting Japan are encouraged to visit to develop your folding skills!

Address	: 1396 Nakatsuhara, Mikicho, Fukuyama City, Hiroshima Prefecture 720-0004, Japan
Phone & Fax	: 084-961-0665
Email	: info@oriplane.com
Admission	: 100 yen—less than $1 US (for ages 3 and up)
Hours	: Every Saturday from 10:00 AM to 4:00 PM (for weekday and public holiday visits, please consult in advance via email or phone).

Toyomatsu Paper Airplane Tower

In the spring of 2003, the world's first paper airplane-dedicated tower was completed at the summit of Yonami Mountain, which is 2,175 feet (663 m) above sea level, in Jinsekikogen, Hiroshima. The steel structure has two floors, with an 85-foot (26-m) high observation deck on top. The first floor has a room for making paper airplanes, from which visitors can ascend to the observation deck. When the tower is open, visitors can fly their own folded paper airplanes from the observation deck. The building incorporates a solar panels on its roof and, together with the wind turbine installed in the park, it supplies its own electricity demands. On March 22, 2003, the first All-Japan Origami Airplane Championship final was held here. There are plans to regularly hold national and world championships.

Address	: 381 Shimotoyomatsu, Jinsekikogen Town, Jinseki District, Hiroshima Prefecture 720-1704, Japan
Phone	: 0847-84-2000
Admission	: 300 yen—less than $2 US (elementary school students and up) includes 5 sheets of eco-friendly paper (use of paper other than the provided eco-friendly paper is not permitted).
Hours	: The tower is open Tuesday, Thursday, Saturday, Sunday and public holidays. From April to September, 10:00 AM to 6:00 PM. In October, November and March, 10:00 AM to 5:00 PM. Closed from December to February. Open daily during Golden Week and the summer vacation period (late July to the end of August).

Takuo Toda—Activity Highlights

1976	: Began developing original paper airplanes under the guidance of origami artist Eiji Nakamura.
1993	: Held the first paper airplane exhibition at the Fukuyama Art Museum, attracting 5,721 visitors.
1996	: Organized and supervised paper airplane competitions in Germany, Saga and Kagoshima.
1997	: Conducted a flight experiment from the Arc de Triomphe, broadcasted by Fuji TV.
1998	: Hosted a paper airplane exhibition at the Kawanoe Paper Town Museum in Ehime.
1999	: Successfully flew a nearly 10-foot (3-m) giant airplane, achieving a flight time of 35 seconds and a distance of nearly 443 feet (135 m) (sponsored by Tokai TV, received the Director-General of the Science and Technology Agency Award). Gave a lecture at the Aerospace Fair '99 in Nagoya.
2001	: Opened the Paper Airplane Museum.
2002	: Broke Ken Blackburn's indoor duration record for a pure origami airplane with a new record of 18.1 seconds (from 17.1 seconds).
2003	: Supervised the script and taught Kimura Takuya how to fold and fly paper airplanes for the TBS drama *Good Luck!!* Held the "1st All Japan Origami Airplane Contest."
2004	: Taught paper airplane making in Pokhara, Nepal. Updated the world record at Tokyo Dome (19.24 seconds, broadcasted by Nippon Television). Supervised a paper airplane competition at the INPACT event with the support of the Ministry of Education, Science and Culture of Thailand (80,000 participants, attended by Thai royalty). *The Evolution of Origami Airplanes* (NHK Publishing) was included in the national high school mock exam language questions.
2005	: Held the "2nd All Japan Origami Airplane Contest."
2006	: Cooperated with Hiroshima Prefecture's Dream Delivery Project (giant paper airplane).
2007	: Held the first elementary school invitational tournament.
2008	: Conducted a successful public experiment of space origami airplanes at the University of Tokyo.
2009	: Broke the Guinness World Record for indoor flight duration (27.9 seconds). Sky King was selected as one of the top 50 best inventions by *TIME* magazine in the USA.
2010	: Updated the Guinness World Record for indoor flight duration (29.2 seconds).
2011	: Held a Guinness challenge contest as part of the 100th anniversary of aviation in Tokorozawa. Conducted a project to uplift spirits for the recovery from the Great East Japan Earthquake.
2013	: Contributed as a paper airplane expert on *Shimajiro: A Wonderful Adventure* (Benesse Holdings).
2014	: Participated in a large-scale experiment in Okinawa for the *New Year's Special Gift from Sanma & Tamao!*
2016	: Held the "7th All Japan Origami Airplane Contest" at Todoroki Arena.
2017	: Held the "1st JAL Origami Airplane Asia Contest" at JTA Dome Miyakojima.
2018	: Held the "1st JAL Origami Airplane National Contest" at Ota Ward Gymnasium.

Publications

Fly, Paper Airplane (Japanese and Chinese editions), *Well-Flying Three-Dimensional Origami Airplanes*, *Well-Flying! Origami and Paper Cut Airplanes*, *Playing with Origami Airplanes with Your Child* (all published by Futami Shobo), *The Great Collection of Origami Airplanes BOOK* (Japanese edition / English translation included), *Super Origami Airplanes* (both published by Ikada Publishing), *The Evolution of Origami Airplanes* (NHK Publishing), *Origami Airplanes* (Thai edition) (METC), *Paper Airplane Museum* (edited by the Japan Origami Airplane Association), *Origami Airplane Play* (Showa Grimm), *The World's Best Flying Paper Airplane BOOK* (Takarajimasha), among others.

"Books to Span the East and West"

Tuttle Publishing was founded in 1832 in the small New England town of Rutland, Vermont [USA]. Our core values remain as strong today as they were then—to publish best-in-class books which bring people together one page at a time. In 1948, we established a publishing outpost in Japan—and Tuttle is now a leader in publishing English-language books about the arts, languages and cultures of Asia. The world has become a much smaller place today and Asia's economic and cultural influence has grown. Yet the need for meaningful dialogue and information about this diverse region has never been greater. Over the past seven decades, Tuttle has published thousands of books on subjects ranging from martial arts and paper crafts to language learning and literature—and our talented authors, illustrators, designers and photographers have won many prestigious awards. We welcome you to explore the wealth of information available on Asia at **www.tuttlepublishing.com**.

Published by Tuttle Publishing, an imprint of Periplus Editions (HK) Ltd.

www.tuttlepublishing.com

978-4-8053-1873-7

Kids Origami Hikoki Kyorigata
Copyright © Takuo Toda 2018
English translation rights arranged with Ikada-sha Publishers Co., Ltd.
through Japan UNI Agency, Inc., Tokyo

Printed in China 2410CM
29 28 27 26 25   10 9 8 7 6 5 4 3 2 1

Distributed by:
North America, Latin America & Europe
Tuttle Publishing
364 Innovation Drive
North Clarendon
VT 05759-9436 U.S.A.
Tel: (802) 773-8930
Fax: (802) 773-6993
info@tuttlepublishing.com
www.tuttlepublishing.com

Japan
Tuttle Publishing
Yaekari Building 3rd Floor
5-4-12 Osaki Shinagawa-ku
Tokyo 141 0032
Tel: (81) 3 5437-0171
Fax: (81) 3 5437-0755
sales@tuttle.co.jp
www.tuttle.co.jp

Asia Pacific
Berkeley Books Pte. Ltd.
3 Kallang Sector, #04-01
Singapore 349278
Tel: (65) 6741-2178
Fax: (65) 6741-2179
inquiries@periplus.com.sg
www.tuttlepublishing.com

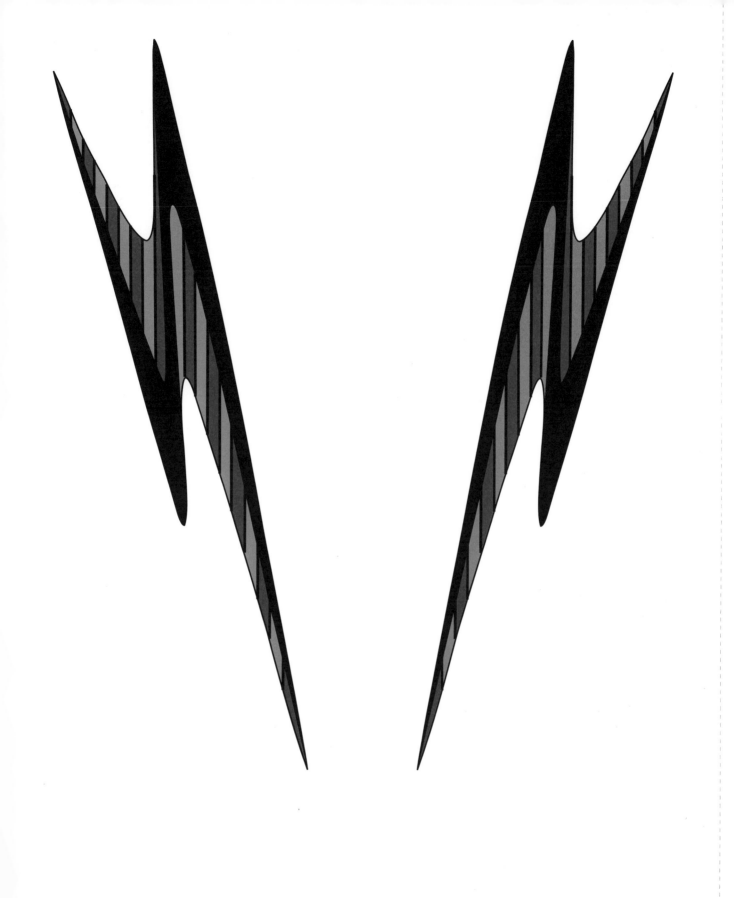

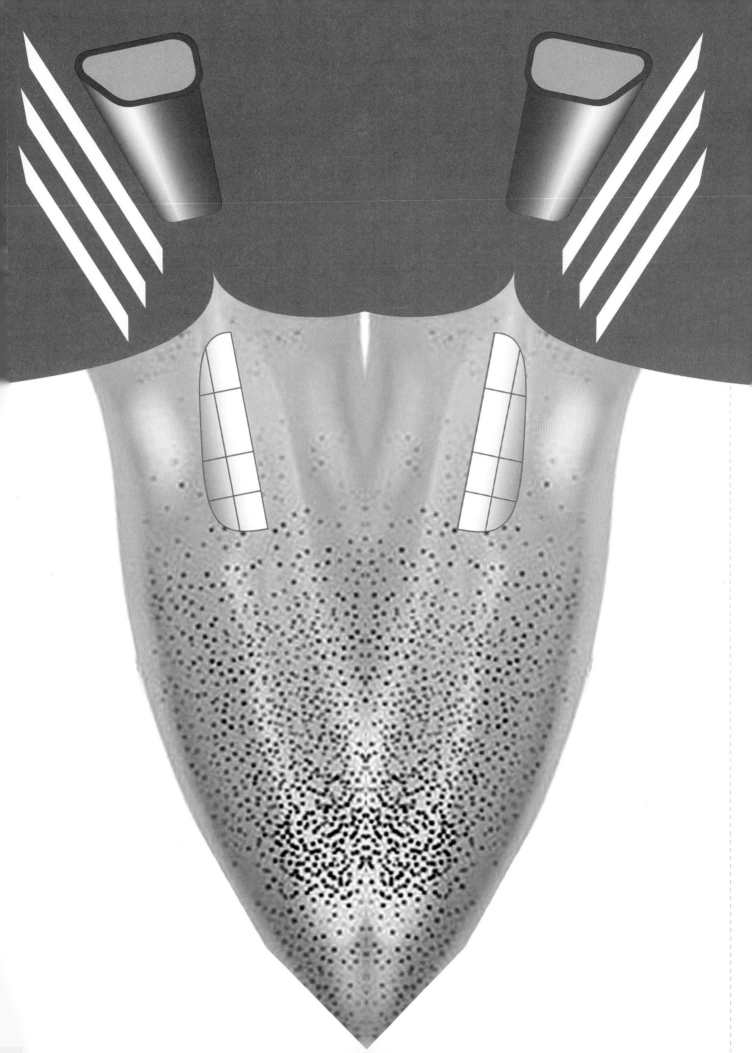

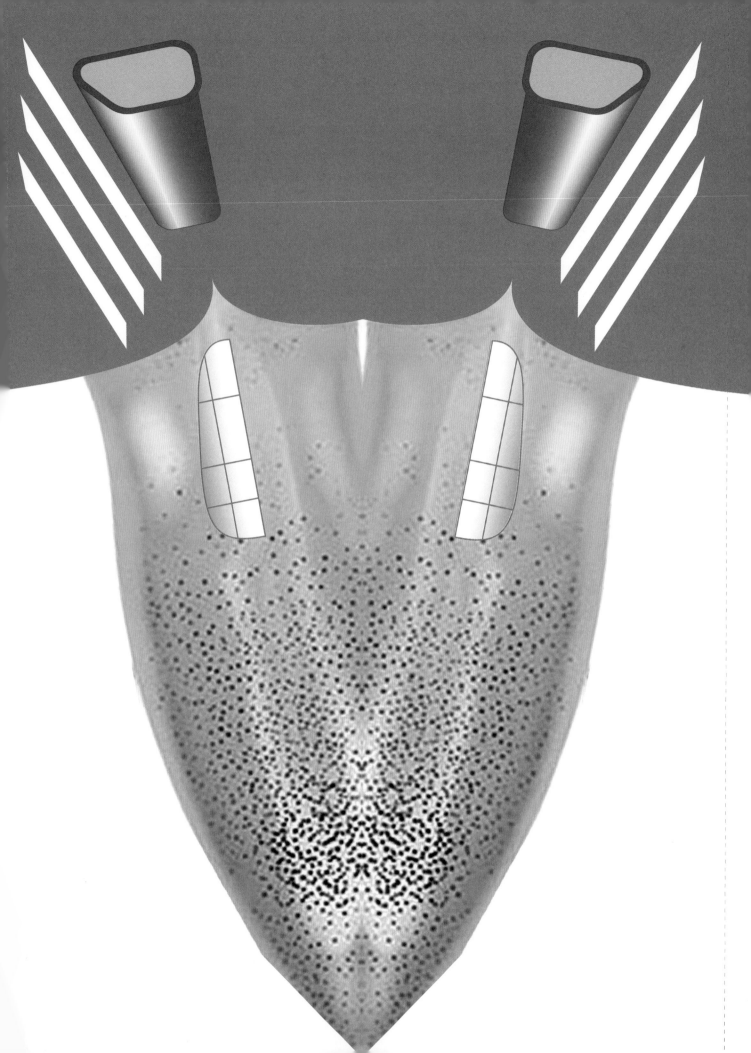

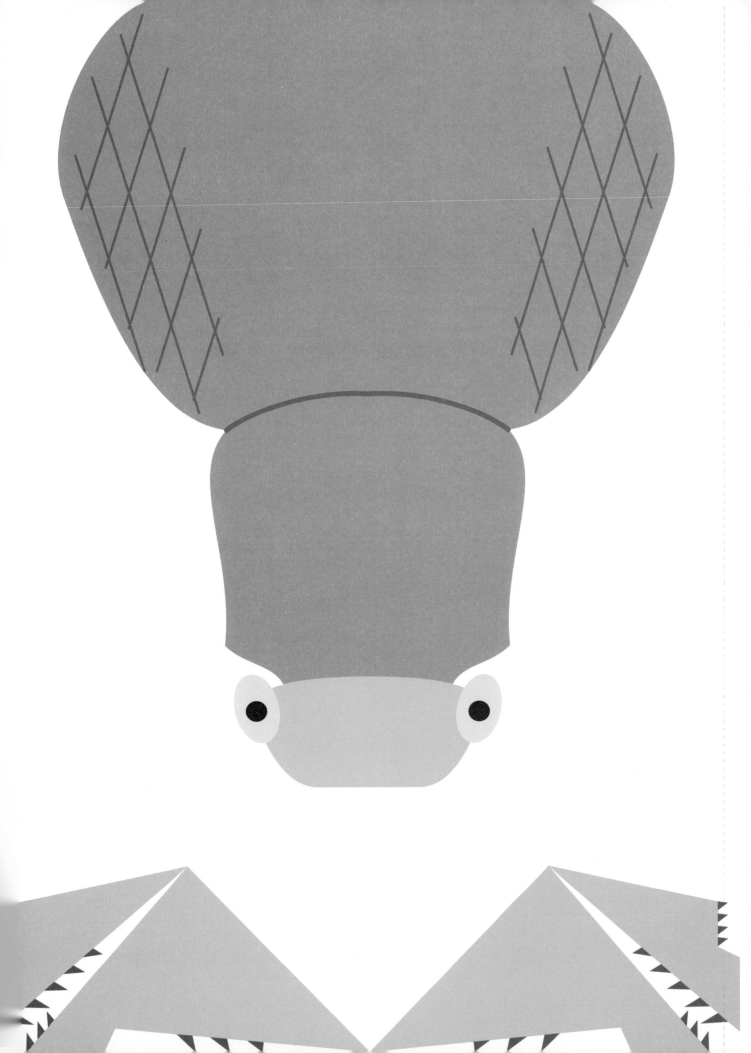

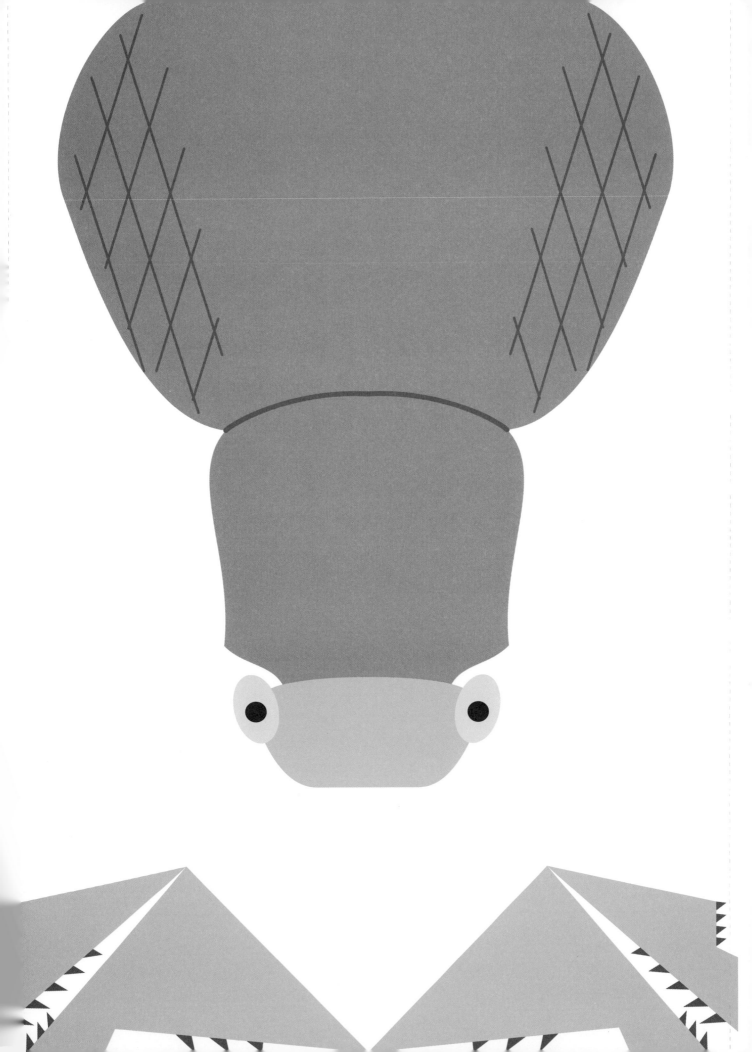

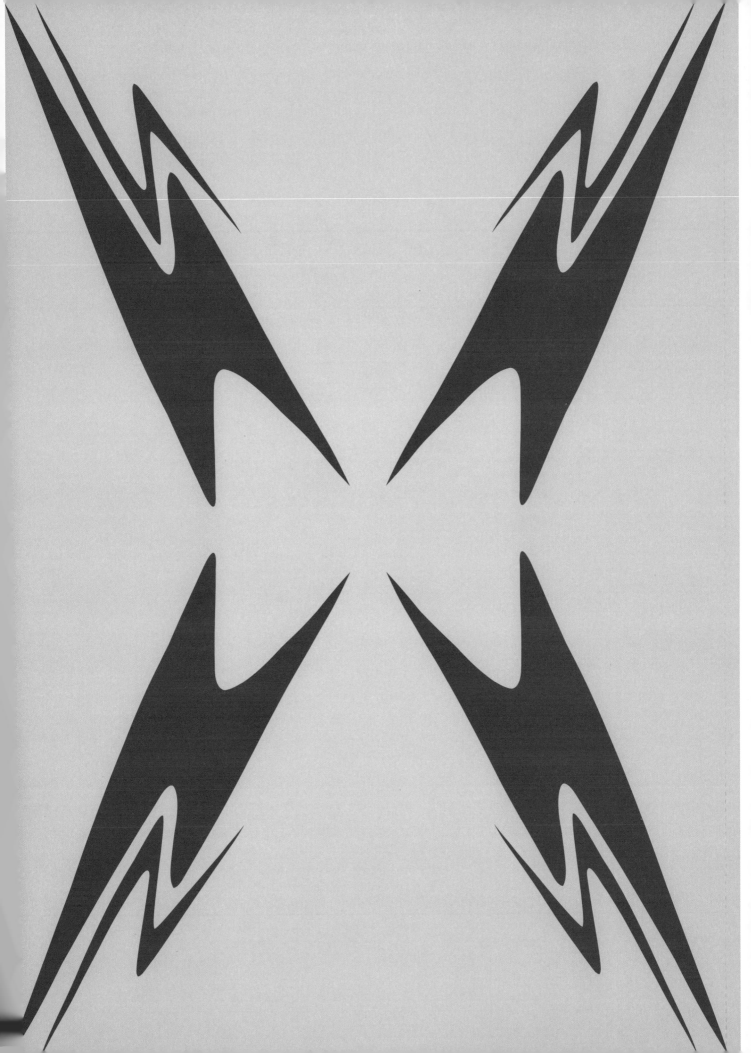

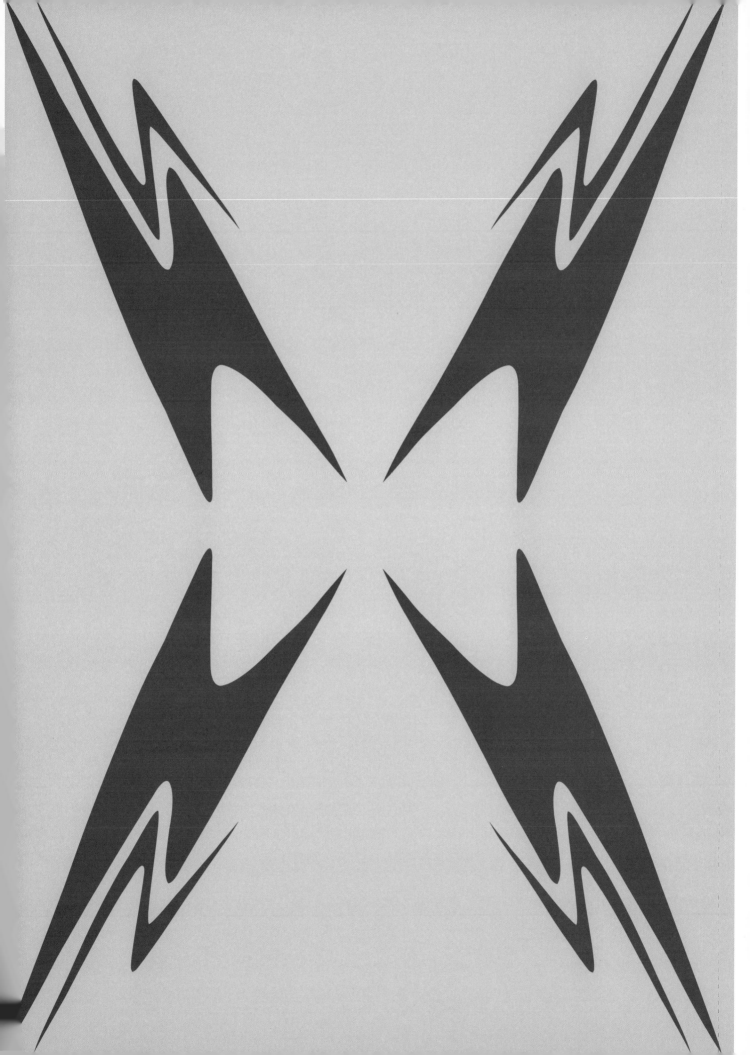

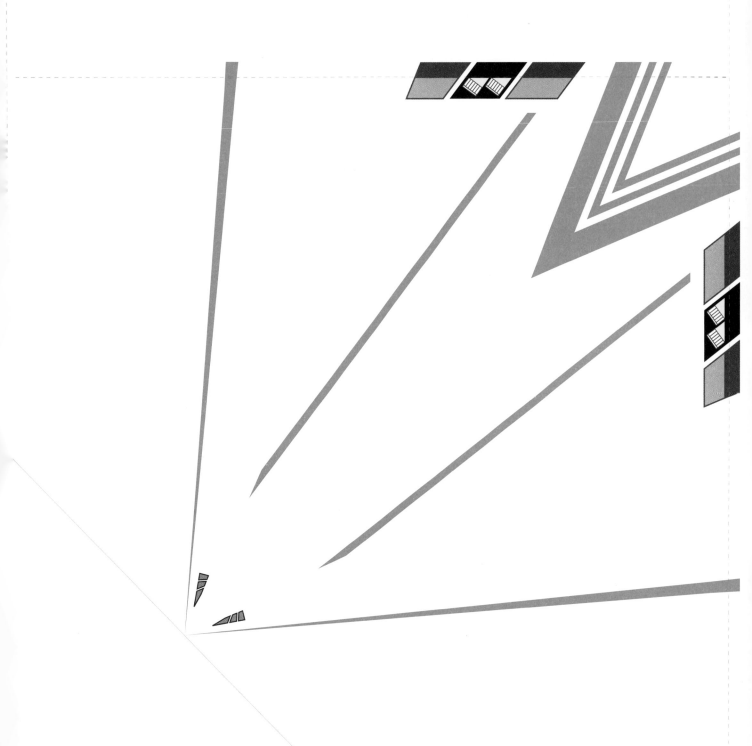

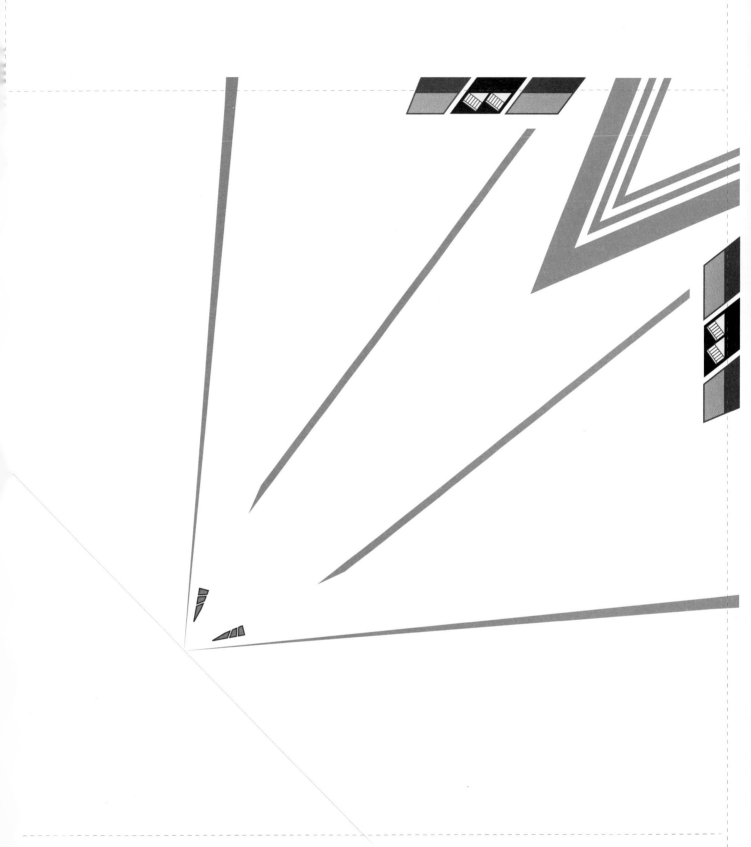

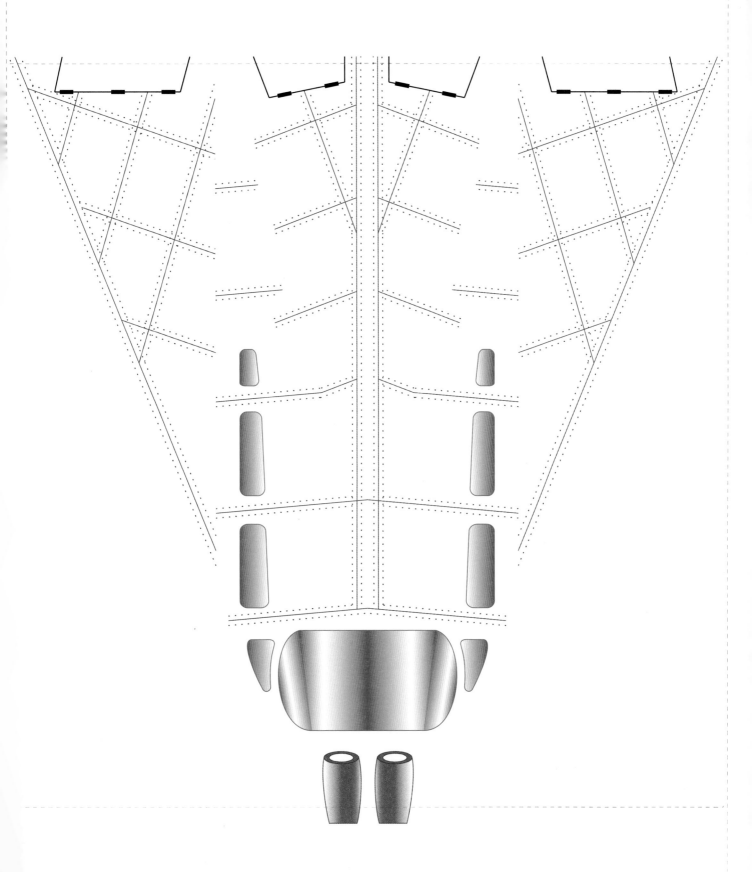

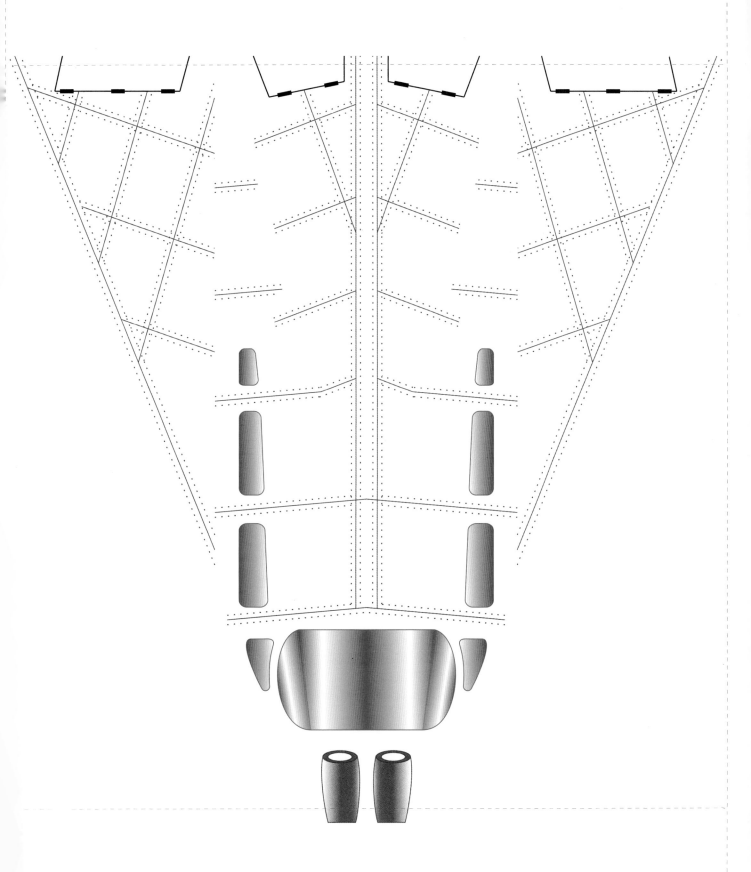

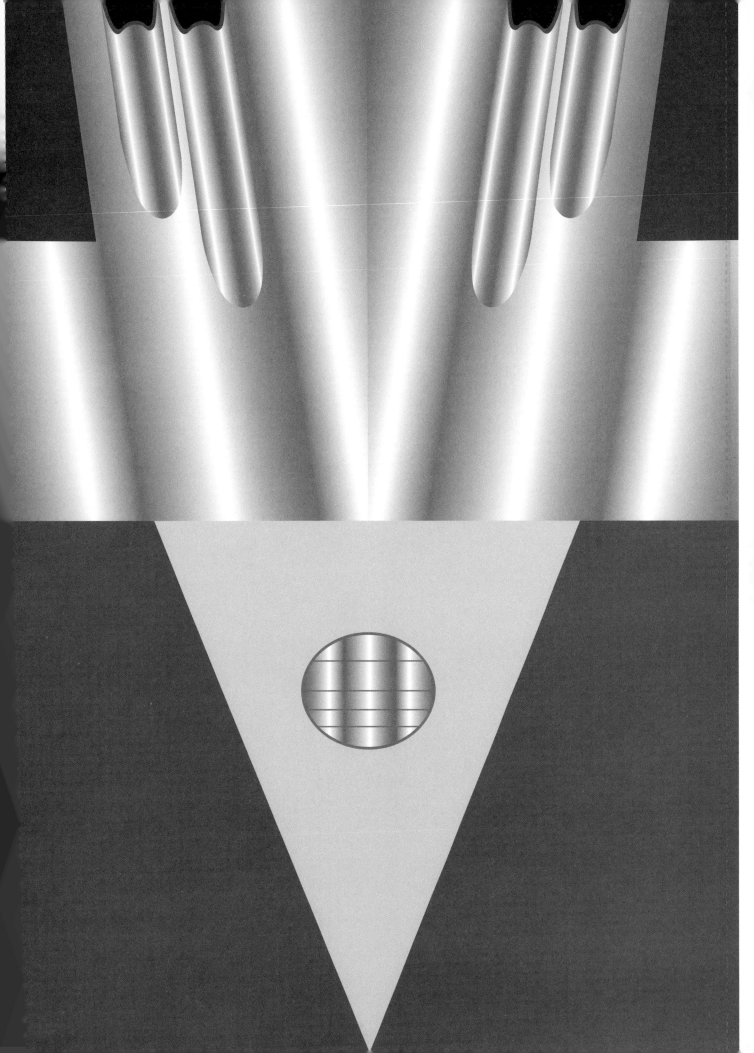

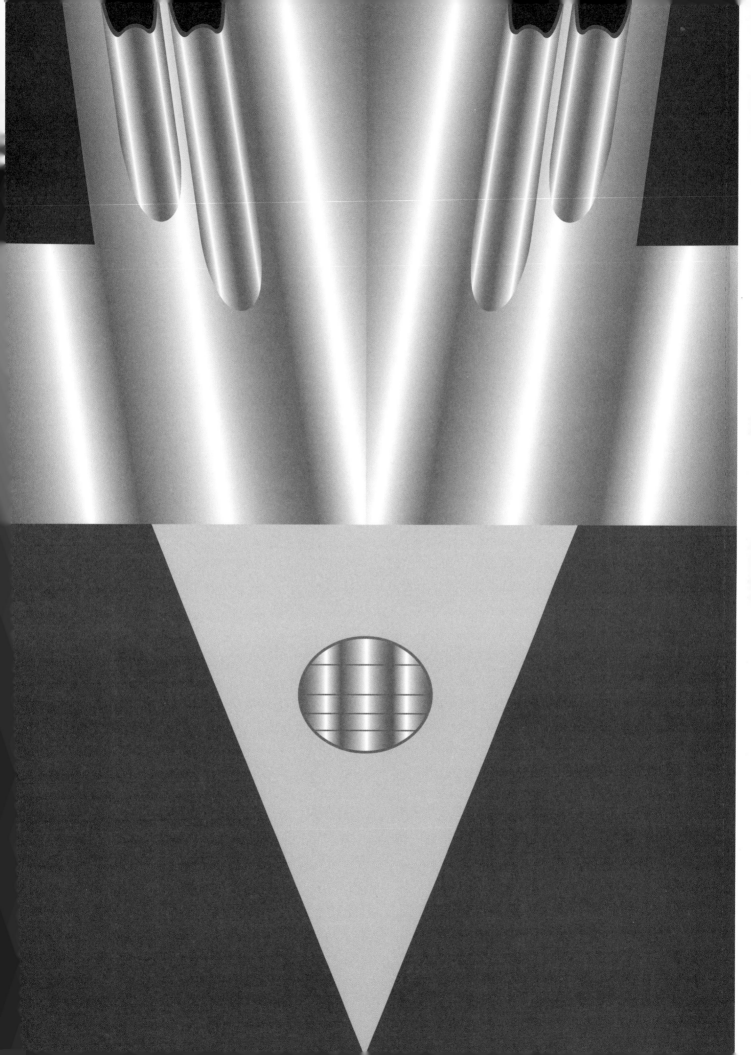